THE ILLUMINATION CODEX
GATEWAY FIVE

Laying of Hands

Reiki & Beyond

Michael Garber

MICHAEL GARBER

Printed in the United States of America
First Printing 2021
First Edition 2021

Second Edition

ISBNs:
Softcover 978-1-959561-15-6
eBook 978-1-959561-16-3

10 9 8 7 6 5 4 3 2 1

THE
ILLUMINATION
CODEX

Table of Contents

ACKNOWLEDGMENTS

I bow in humble recognition of the One Light of Consciousness, the Source of my being and the source of all knowledge and wisdom. I give gratitude to the Supreme for dreaming me into existence and allowing me to have the conscious experience of life and the crafting of this codex.

I bow in love and gratitude to my dear beloved partner Ron Amit, a true gift of the Divine, for all the many ways he supports me in my life. I am blessed beyond measure to have such a brilliant master of love, compassion, and divine service to walk this earthly life with. Thank you for all that you do, seen and unseen, to amplify joy and higher consciousness for me and all beings in the Cosmos. I love you across all space, time, and dimensions.

I send gratitude to my friends and clients who have brought forth the lost stories of Creation through their Illuminated Quantum Healing hypnosis sessions. Thank you for being the powerful Light beacons that you are!

I send deep gratitude to my many modern scribes who assisted me in the transcription work. Thank you for helping me capture these incredible client stories so that the world can remember our cosmic divine heritage.

Bless all the beings, seen and unseen, who have helped me craft this material so that you, the reader, can be nourished on your path of Ascension. May you, the reader, be blessed infinitely and discover the highest truth of your being. May ascended consciousness, liberation, and divine unification be yours in this very life!

DEDICATION AND INVOCATION

This book is dedicated to the infinite expressions of our Oneself, for the celebration of our many incarnations, past, present, and future, and the lessons we have learned throughout eternity. May these words and the energy they carry be a potent force for awakening for all seekers of Unconditional Love and divine Truth. May this transmission support the reactivation and restoration of humanity's divine blueprint upon planet Earth and accelerate the realization of our eternal unity and oneness with all of Creation.

Let us join in prayer, honoring and sending gratitude to the Supreme Intelligent Source of Creation, the omniscient, omnipotent, omnipresent, transcendental Divine Source that is our True Nature.

Let us honor and send gratitude to the higher Light realms and the beings of Light who guide and protect Creation's evolution. Let us honor and send gratitude to our star lineages and those who support us from beyond the Earth. Let us receive your love and blessings now as we remember our cosmic ancestry and our role in the higher evolutionary plan for Creation.

Let us honor and send gratitude to our Earth Mother and her many dimensions and manifestations of Life including the animal, plant, bacterial, fungal, protozoan, mineral, crystalline, and elemental beings who contribute to her dynamic, regenerative biomes. These writings are offered as salve and balm to heal and bless our beloved Gaia, our Earth Mother and Divine Sister. May her waters be pure, her soil rich, her air clean, and may all beings, seen and unseen, within her living biofield know lasting peace forever and ever.

Let us honor and send gratitude to the wisdom and guidance from the seven directions of East, South, West, North, Above, Below, and Within. Let us call back our soul fragments scattered through time and space so that we may anchor ourselves HERE and NOW in this eternal moment of infinite potential to witness the unfolding manifestation of the Divine Plan.

Let us honor and send gratitude to the elements of Earth, Air, Fire, Water, and Ether that create the foundation of our evolutionary experience in form. May the Light of Consciousness awaken swiftly in each of us as we remember our True Nature beyond names and forms.

Let us honor and send gratitude to our ancestors and the many souls who have shared their light upon the Earth. Let us send special thanks to those who dedicated their lives to passing on the Mysteries and sacred knowledge of the Divine so that we may NOW stand at this Grand Turning of the Ages, with the support of all who have come and all who are destined to live upon this great Earth.

I call forth the full remembering of our divinity and the weaving of a new story of harmony and peace for all of Life upon the Earth. May we shed our stories of limitation and suffering and step forward into a new era as People of Light, cosmic co-citizens, and ambassadors for the Living Light of Creation.

Hallelujah! Jai! Aho! Blessed Be! Amen! And so, it is! Om!

GUIDANCE FOR READING THIS BOOK

The Illumination Codex is a multidimensional library for the path of Ascension. It is holographic by nature as each chapter contains a multitude of keycodes to activate ancient cellular memory and trigger multidimensional awareness and higher consciousness integration. As you read the material, your Inner Being will offer flashes of insight and higher perception into your awareness to assist you in healing, spiritual activation, and cosmic remembrance. I recommend using a highlighter, journaling your process, and using other resources to research and enhance your understanding of the topics presented in this book.

A major influence for this material comes from my work as a past-life regression hypnotherapist using the methods we have codified into a technique called Illuminated Quantum Healing (IQH). While in a deep hypnotic trance, my clients experience other lifetimes and other planetary civilizations and communicate with advanced intelligent species from beyond the Earth and Earth plane. The information contained in this book is a summary of my understanding of all that I have learned through my clients as they journeyed to the ancient past, probable timelines of the future, and higher planes of Light. There are many transcriptions of IQH sessions included in the book for you to have your own unique interpretation and multidimensional experience with the material.

This book contains a diverse collection of spiritual information from a variety of wisdom traditions that I have studied in my life. These writings are my own interpretations and understandings of these different concepts that have helped me in my awakening journey and do not necessarily speak for the lineages themselves. This presentation of information is meant as a collection of keys to unlock the wisdom that is already encoded within you. None of it is meant to become dogmatic as consciousness revelation and ascendency will open us continuously to higher and higher truths and understanding.

I confess that I share this transmission as a fellow traveler on the path of awakening. I have my own limitations, my own egoic nature, and my own struggles. I am capable of error and ignorance just as any other person. This presentation of information is what I have found along my path which has triggered awakening and helped me on my path back home to my Self. My prayer is that this book will become deeply meaningful for you and be a guiding light back to your own liberated being.

While reading this material, you may come across something in the text that triggers something within you that is uncomfortable. Maybe it is words that I use, perspectives that I share, or something else that may bring up resistance, judgment, anger, guilt, and so on. This is a wonderful opportunity to investigate the origin of the reactive mental and emotional patterns that create such experiences. The origin may come from earlier stages of your life or previous lifetimes. Use this as an opportunity to reconcile those parts of your consciousness through spiritual inquiry and self-study so that you may realize deeper states of wholeness and clarity.

This text is intended to activate 'gnosis,' a direct experience and knowledge of the divine presence within and around you. I do not recommend blind faith in any concept or religious doctrine. The information in this book is not meant to be treated as religious dogma that cannot be questioned or developed further. It is meant to be utilized to unlock the truth that lives within your very being. I am not writing this intending to change people's beliefs or convert anyone. I am simply relaying the summary of my life's research on the quest for spiritual truth. If something from the material does not resonate as truth in your heart, release it and move on to the next part of the transmission. Use the philosophy and information in this text to stimulate your expansion and the embodiment of YOUR deepest truth and to strengthen your relationship and innate connection with the Divine.

Another thing to mention is capitalization. You will notice that there are words that are not normally capitalized in other books and sacred texts that are capitalized in this text. My intention behind this was to add spiritual dimensionality to words that describe qualities or names of the Divine.

Typically, when I speak of light in this book, I am speaking about higher-dimensional, intelligently-encoded subtle energy and not conventional light from a light bulb. When I speak about "energy," I am speaking about subtle energy which exists beyond the visible light spectrum for most people. Many are becoming sensitive to subtle energy (i.e., multisensory, intuitive, psychic) and are developing the ability to sense and perceive this energy through extrasensory perception. All of humanity is evolving towards being able to perceive and interact with subtle energy and higher cosmic intelligence and consciousness.

The use of the term consciousness fluctuates throughout the book and can mean different things. When I speak of pure Consciousness I am speaking about your True Self as Source Consciousness, the Absolute, the Eternal Witness of all Creation, pure Awareness and Existence itself. Other times I will speak of consciousness as in variations of the mind such as unity consciousness or separation consciousness. All forms of consciousness, all experiences of the mind, borrow existence from the One Light of Consciousness and you are that!

I tried my best to organize this text in a way that can be read from front to back like any regular book, but it can also be read any way you feel intuitively called to read it. Part of the reason for the size of this codex is because it is difficult to explain one part without understanding many other components. In my effort to answer all potential and probable questions about ascension, I wrote everything I could on this multifaceted, multidimensional topic.

As you make your journey through this material, there are three stages to help integrate the information and use it to fuel your awakening to your True Nature:

Stage One: Listening (*Sravana*) As you read or listen to the material in this book, allow it to penetrate deeply and work with your inner philosophical understanding. Listen deeply to your Inner Being for there will be flashes of insight and knowing that emerge within your inner consciousness space.

Stage Two: Reflection (*Manana*) Try your best to understand the information contained in this book through self-inquiry and inner philosophical pondering. I am not asking for you to blindly believe any of this transmission. Think of this information as an active hypothesis. You do not have to believe it, but you can reflect over the information and see how it applies to your life.

Stage Three: Integration/Meditation (*Nididhyasana*) As you take in the words in stage one and convert the words to knowledge and understanding in stage two, you move into conviction and integration of knowledge in stage three as you crystallize and embody the Self-knowledge of "I am Pure Consciousness." As you go about your daily life, use the knowledge you have gained to interrupt habit and conditioned thought and re-direct your mind toward the Light of Consciousness that you are.

Gateways of Entry

Besides reading front-to-back or intuitively hopping around, I have created six gateways for you to enter the presentation of the material. I have created one large book that has all of the Illumination Codex material and separated the material into separately published volumes to make the information more digestible. The Gateways are as follows:

GATEWAY ONE: ASCENSION INITIATION: KEYS FOR HIGHER EVOLUTION gives an overall understanding of Ascension, reincarnation, universal law, and a theoretical and philosophical framework concerning Cosmic Evolution. This is an excellent place to start if you are open and eager to learn about these subjects and awakening, you may want to start in Gateway Three.

GATEWAY TWO: AKASHIC DATABASE contains a wide variety of Illuminated Quantum Healing session transcriptions describing key figures and events in the history of Creation, galactic history, ancient planetary history, and probable future timelines of New Earth from clients in hypnotic visionary states. This is a suitable place to enter the material if you already have a general understanding of multidimensionality, galactic civilizations, and the process of personal and planetary ascension. This gateway is conveniently separated into QUANTUM ORIGINS, COSMIC CHRIST TRANSMISSIONS, and NEW EARTH TRANSMISSIONS. If you find yourself resistant to those ideas and are new to these subjects. I recommend developing a meditation practice parallel to reading this material as the transcripts are deeply activating on multiple levels.

GATEWAY THREE: PATH OF AWAKENING: KEYS FOR TRANSFIGURATION is an in-depth collection of spiritual and philosophical wisdom to support personal, relational, and planetary healing. If you are in the beginning stages of awakening or moving through a deep healing process, you may wish to start here so you can develop your consciousness and prepare your mind and body for higher level initiation into the Mysteries.

GATEWAY FOUR: CHAKRA YOGA DISCOURSE transmits deeper

insight into the themes and physio-psycho-spiritual domains of the vortices of life force and perception called the *chakras*. Each section transmits valuable information to understand the common distortions in these processing centers and how to activate and reconcile each center.

GATEWAY FIVE: LAYING HANDS: REIKI & BEYOND is a full manual for learning the art of the laying of hands for healing. The manual clearly describes all the stages, steps, and practices to perform powerfully transformative hands-on-healing sessions for yourself, others, and even in groups. This manual would be acceptable for any Level 1 and Level 2 Reiki course.

GATEWAY SIX: ASCENSION LEXICON is a glossary of commonly used words to describe the process of awakening and ascension. These definitions act as keycode activators to unlock deeper meaning and inner wisdom. Many words used in spiritual/ascension circles are convoluted and sometimes lose their impact because they are misused or misunderstood. I may use words in a way you are not familiar with, or I may use words differently than you. I tried my best to make a glossary with foundational vocabulary to assist with understanding the material. You may wish to read the ASCENSION LEXICON before journeying through the main text of the book.

Bless you on your personal path through this material. May the light in your heart guide you with ease and grace on your journey of initiation with *The Illumination Codex*.

Awakening to the Quantum Reality

In the Summer of 2016, I was given a book that forever changed my life's direction called *The Three Waves of Volunteers and the New Earth* by Dolores Cannon. This book was a huge catalyst in my spiritual awakening. Reading the text stirred something deep within me and resonated profoundly with my heart's truth. The book's pages sent waves of energy down my spine as I began to awaken to a higher consciousness reality and remember my purpose for being born upon the Earth at this time.

Dolores Cannon was a world-renowned hypnotherapist specializing in past-life regression. To understand the power of regressive hypnosis, we also need to understand the workings of the mind. The mind can be separated into three categories: the conscious mind, the subconscious mind, and the superconscious mind.

The conscious mind is the ego/personality part of the mind. This active part of the mind uses limited information from the environment and past experiences to make decisions and take care of the body.

The subconscious mind is the recording device of our mind. It records incredible amounts of information at every moment. We easily pull data from the subconscious when we think about something from our past as we access memory.

Deeper in the subconscious, sometimes called the unconscious mind, we have unconscious memories and information, including societal conditioning, painful traumas from this life that are too painful to remember, and memories from other lifetimes. Even though this information is not in the conscious mind, it silently influences our day-to-day experience as reactive emotional momentum, called *samskaras* in Sanskrit, from past events which overlay and filter our experience of the present moment. These subconscious patterns are like applications running in the background of smartphones that quietly drain the processing speed and battery, silently influencing processor speed and functionality.

The superconscious mind is a higher mind capacity that gives us access to intuitive information, extrasensory perception, non-local consciousness, creative genius, universal connection, and access to divine consciousness. This part of the mind is mostly undiscovered and underdeveloped in most of humanity.

Dolores created a unique method of hypnosis, Quantum Healing Hypnosis Technique (QHHT), that opened a doorway to the client's subconscious mind to explore other lifetimes and realms in Creation. When I use the word "quantum," I am speaking to the fabric of Consciousness, the multidimensional unified field of Creation. When clients are in these hypnotic states, they tap into the part of their consciousness that is nonlocal and connected to All That Is. This includes access to other lifetimes, other realities and dimensions, and other intelligent consciousness forms (i.e., higher-dimensional light beings, telepathic extraterrestrials, etc.). Through this experience, clients came to understand another perspective and origin of self-sabotaging and limiting beliefs that were playing out in this life and the core mental/emotional patterns that create illness and disease.

During her sessions, Dolores started to contact a part of her clients' consciousness that seemed to have endless knowledge and wisdom. She called this aspect of her clients the Subconscious or the SC. Others have called this the Higher Self, the oversoul, superconsciousness, or the cosmic consciousness. I prefer the term Higher Self and superconscious mind and go into great detail of how to activate and evolve superconsciousness throughout this text. While the information was limitless, the SC/Higher Self would only answer questions in a way that was appropriate for the client's learning path and honored their free will. When working with the SC, both Dolores and the client described powerful healing energy in their bodies and the treatment room. Clients often reported instantaneous healing as they were transformed from the inside out during the session. While this may seem too good to be true, there are countless documented and measurable occurrences where clients received lasting miraculous healing through these types of sessions.

When she would work with the Higher Self, this higher consciousness identity and supportive Light team would speak through the client as a collective consciousness as if the client were speaking in third-person perspective about themselves. "We are always guiding her. We wish she would follow her intuition more." and "We are beginning to use white light to heal this now." are common examples of how "They" (i.e., SC/Higher Self) express themselves and heal the client during the session.

The healing work is always done with unconditional love and honors the free will and sovereignty of the client. If instantaneous healing was not "appropriate" for the client's growth and spiritual maturation, "They" would suggest what steps the client should take to heal themself. Slowly, over many years, Dolores's work expanded as "They" introduced more components to the healing process so that she could evolve her work and teach it to others.

The Three Waves of Volunteers and the New Earth was one of nineteen books written by Dolores Cannon before her transition out of physical life. Each book contains transcriptions of client sessions describing detailed events from other lives while using her Quantum Healing Hypnosis Technique (QHHT).

Awakening to the Starseed Volunteer Mission

After several years of working with clients worldwide, Dolores noticed a pattern of clients describing a massive galactic and higher dimensional mission to raise the vibration of the planet and shift it into a new reality called the New Earth. The book describes how countless numbers of advanced spiritual beings from distant star systems, and even other universes, volunteered to incarnate on the Earth with a mission to raise consciousness on the planet and assist with this grand transition.

The New Earth is a higher frequency Earth reality that exists in a higher dimension than we are in now. Clients describe a large-scale plan initiated by Source Intelligence (God) to reset life on planet Earth back to the original template of a harmonic environment thriving within diversity. Parallel to this, Dolores's work described a shift in human consciousness from a duality-based mindset to a heart-centered, multidimensional consciousness and a less physical body of light.

The First Wave Volunteers were born beginning around 1945 through the 1970s. They were like a stealthy reconnaissance mission. First on the scene. First to patrol and feel out the collective consciousness vibrations. First to introduce the higher consciousness perspectives to the masses. Many had a difficult and lonely time since there were not many other humans in higher, love-based spiritual consciousness on the planet at the time.

The Second Wave Volunteers were born around the late 1970s through

1990s and are channels for higher spiritual energy and divine wisdom. These souls came in with a higher level of intuitive gifts and are often extremely sensitive to energy. Many are hands-on healers, musicians, vocalists, yoga teachers, and so on. They are space-holders who transmit a new frequency out to the field of Earth, bridging the old ways with the new ways and consciousness of New Earth.

The Third Wave Volunteers, the younger generations, are builders and innovative geniuses in science, spirituality, technology, and so on. They are divinely inspired visionaries that will build the New Earth. They are radical lovers and shine bright with crystalline eyes and have achieved high consciousness levels in other lifetimes. Some of these souls have never had a physical incarnation or have come straight from Source as new souls with pure Light and no karma.

I have been told all the children born at this time are part of this Grand Mission. They are pure souls, evolutionary masters, here to build the New Earth. More is written about the Starseed Mission and phenomena later in this book.

As I was reading Dolores's book, I felt I was reading my own story. I felt the truth in her words. Suddenly so many things made sense about my life. I finally had answers to why I felt so different from others in my community and family. I understood why I felt other people's emotions and could tell what people were thinking. It all started to click together. I was so excited to share the book with Ron, my husband and co-founder of New Earth Ascending, who also deeply resonated with the material.

At the same time, we were beginning to work with an Australian musical group as dancers for their "Return of the Bird Tribes" tour for their album by the same name. Something about the term "bird tribes" caught my attention, and I started to research it. I found the book by the same name, written by Ken Carey, in 1988 that describes a prophecy of high spiritual beings returning to the Earth at a time of spiritual renewal.

Many cultures describe times when culture-bringing beings would come from the heavens or from across the waters to bring technology and information to humanity throughout history. Thoth went to the Egyptians, White Buffalo Calf Woman went to the Native Americans, Quetzalcoatl went to the Aztecs, the Seven Sisters of the Pleiades went to the Aboriginal people of Australia, beings from the Sirius A and B binary star system went to the Dogon people of Mali; and many other stories exist in many other cultures. Carey's book described when these beings would come again during a time of spiritual awakening on the planet.

I was receiving information from multiple directions and was going through a massive realignment with my soul's purpose as I became aware of this greater story and mission. Ron and I went to an arts festival in the desert of Nevada called Burning Man. While we were there, a couple excitedly recognized us as "twin flames" and asked us which star system we had come from. "We are from Sirius. Where are you from? Orion? The Pleiades? Sirius?" she asked. The concept of "starseeds" and "twin flames" was new to me, and I did not know what to say. I saw a special sparkle in the couple's eyes and felt that I should do some research to understand more about it.

After some research and some magical synchronicities, Ron convinced me that we should do the QHHT training and certification process. I was super resistant to learning it because of deep religious programming and egoic structures that made me doubtful of the truthfulness of the work. I was familiar with reincarnation but did not necessarily believe in it. Eventually, I gave in to Ron's suggestion and took the QHHT course.

Evolving Beyond QHHT

In the early stages of practicing QHHT, Ron and I were guided to start doing the sessions online to share the technique's power with as many people as we could. This method was not permitted by the organization because Dolores did not believe it to be safe and her organization does not permit it still. Dolores was an elder and this type of technology was new to her, whereas the younger generations are much more comfortable interfacing with video conferencing.

We have been told by the Higher Consciousness that there is nothing to fear, and NOW is the time to spread these healing methods across the world in whatever way is possible. To honor our lineage and teacher, we stopped using the name QHHT and started experimenting with different names as our way of practicing quantum healing evolved beyond our initial training.

Online sessions are just as powerful as in-person sessions and are often more comfortable and affordable for the client. It is completely safe to facilitate sessions remotely, and we have had countless powerful sessions that have been facilitated in this way. Dolores's organization does not allow adaptation of the QHHT technique. Its practitioners need to perform the method exactly how Dolores taught and not add any modifications or outside techniques. While it is important to protect the work's integrity, this rigidity does not permit the work to expand to its full potential. We are in a time of expansion and evolution, and we must always be open to the transformation and progression of all methods we currently use or risk leaving them in the past as everything on the Earth is evolving.

Another topic that caused us to evolve beyond our initial training of QHHT was the organization's strict denial of negative spiritual attachment and what felt like shaming those who believed in this common experience. Ron and I and other quantum healing practitioners discovered that certain psychological, emotional, and physical imbalances were being created by pervasive energies that did not belong to the client's energy field that had somehow become attached to the client. This includes spirit attachments, curses from past lives, and implants from nefarious beings to name a few. QHHT did not provide us with appropriate training to work with these serious complications. If it were found out that a practitioner had adopted these practices and still operated under the name of QHHT, practitioners could be removed from the QHHT directory.

Many practitioners have reported spontaneous visitation from Dolores through clients under hypnosis where she has encouraged practitioners to follow their intuitive guidance and continue to develop the work through experimentation just as she did when she developed QHHT.

We were inspired greatly by other quantum healing practitioners' extraction methods and crafted our own approaches to clearing pervasive energies and spirit attachments. The reality of negative thought-forms, negative extraterrestrial implants, and entity attachment is too big to ignore, considering so many cases are emerging, not to forget the thousands of years of wisdom and extraction practices passed down by Indigenous peoples and various wisdom traditions.

We never assume that someone has an entity just because they suffer, and we do not bring it up in our intake interview. Once the client is deep in a hypnotic trance, we ask the Higher Self if there are entities or attached energies. If the answer is yes, then we ask questions to understand how this occurred and if the client has anything to learn to release negative attachment. From there, the Higher Self can immediately extract the energy and take it back into the Light for healing. It is all extremely safe, insightful, and benefits all who are involved. We have found that, often, the revelation of spirit attachment or implants will not occur unless the practitioner asks and gives permission for a scan specifically for attached energies. Ron and I believe this is because of the honoring of the free will of the entities involved in the experience of attachment.

In my opinion, to continue to deny such experiences is a disservice to the clients who come to us seeking answers and healing. All practices and traditions can become dogmatic if we do not allow the evolution of thought to take us into new frontiers of consciousness. These are evolutionary practices, and we need to be constantly open to shifting our paradigm so that we can offer the best guidance and support with the changing of times.

Once we started offering quantum healing sessions online, clients started coming to Ron and me from all over the world. Not only were the sessions powerfully healing and transformative for the clients, but we were also going through a rapid transformation as we learned about ancient stories and galactic events from the perspective of souls embodied at those times. While Dolores taught that many people had "potato-picking lives," simple lives with simple themes, it seemed that almost every session of mine had to do with the New Earth Mission, powerful events from the ancient past, and future timelines of Earth.

I soon realized that I was getting a theme and timeline in my sessions. The timeline given to me via my clients describes how Creation came into being, ancient galactic history, the seeding of life on Earth, the rise and fall of ancient civilizations, the true teachings of Jesus through the eyes of people that were closest to him, information about the transformation of the human body to a less dense body of Light, and the evolution of the Earth into the higher frequency reality of New Earth. In less than a year, I went from a reincarnation skeptic to believing that anything is possible, and that the multiverse is more incredible than we can even imagine!

Illuminated Quantum Healing

After years of practicing and evolving how we do this work, Ron and I have created our own quantum healing method that incorporates all that we have learned on our path. This includes facilitating sessions online to reach as many people as possible to assist in this Great Awakening.

Our training method acknowledges spirit attachment and teaches our facilitators how to perform negative spirit releasement. We teach yogic psychology, holistic wellness concepts, and energy healing methods to ensure the practitioner has a thorough understanding of human consciousness and how to lead the client through the ascension process using multiple IQH sessions and mentorship programs. We call our method Illuminated Quantum Healing. IQH can be learned in live classes or through our online course offered on our social network Source⊙Energy.

Illuminated Quantum Healing (IQH) is a personal transformation method for multidimensional holistic healing and consciousness development. IQH incorporates energy healing, meditative practices, yogic philosophy, and hypnosis skills to reconcile limiting subconscious patterning and integrate instantaneous multidimensional healing and wisdom from one's Higher Self.

I am deeply honored to be a part of this work. I am so blessed to have an opportunity to work with such incredible people and energies. Each session that I facilitate nourishes me to the core, and I have the sublime opportunity to observe miraculous instantaneous healing and transformation in my clients. After witnessing the infinite potential of quantum healing hypnosis, I firmly believe that we can ascend beyond all states of illness and disease and that we have infinite support to move beyond the shadows of our past and become a new People of Light.

Getting to the New Earth involves a process of spiritual growth and purification. To transition with the Earth, it is required that we raise our vibration to match the accelerating frequency of the Earth as it changes. Mostly, this is about releasing fear and negative karma. I have written this book as a tool to use for your spiritual awakening and transformation that many are calling Ascension. This is my gift to humanity to help make the process easier and explain different components to cultivate a deeper understanding of this Grand Shift to New Earth and our newly evolving Lightbody.

Spiritual awakening and ascension are available for ALL people no matter what they have done in their past, current economic status, gender expression, sexuality, religion, etc. There are as many paths to the New Earth as there are humans on the planet. No one religion holds the keys or the way to heaven. The power is within YOU!

To support the global ascension process, we have created New Earth Ascending. New Earth Ascending is a non-profit, faith-based organization focused on global ascension and establishing heart-centered, sustainable communities and educational centers around the world.

Alongside Illuminated Quantum Healing (IQH), Ron and I have created other pathways of support for the global ascension process:

1.   Embodied Light Reiki Training and Certification

2.   New Earth Ascending has three levels of Reiki certification to train people how to channel divine light for healing. These trainings honor the lineage and teachings of the Usui System of Natural Healing while also infusing evolutionary concepts and practices that go beyond standard Reiki training.

3.   Online courses for awakening and ascension are available on our private social network Source◉Energy. The courses include philosophical exploration on several models of spiritual growth and alchemical practices to support your healing, awakening, and ascension. These courses include meditations, holistic wellness education, breathwork, lightbody activation and more. These courses lay foundational understanding for beginners and move through a progression of intermediate and advanced practices and knowledge.

4.   TransformOtion was created to support the embodiment of one's Higher Self using dance, somatic movement, yogic practices, meditation, imagination, and energy healing. This fusion of practices helps to purify and repair the physical, etheric, and mental bodies so that one can move beyond perceived limitations into boundless rhythm and flow. Through this interweaving of multiple disciplinary paths, we integrate physicality with transcendental ecstatic play while cultivating a deep connection with and trust in the body's wisdom.

These ideas and concepts can be used for personal embodiment and activation or infused into performance art to create powerful alchemical experiences for the performer and the audience. This fusion of high art and spiritual transformation creates a multidimensional experience for all who are within the field of performance energies.

5. Source⊙Energy is a social network exclusively for those on the path of ascension to connect and share inspiration as we manifest and build a New Earth. We invite all souls who feel aligned with New Earth to join this network and add your unique energy and love to this community. Source⊙Energy serves as a pathway of social interaction and is the home of our online courses and training.

6. Children are our future. Youth inspiration and enrichment programming is in development to assist the spiritual activation and consciousness mastery of the youth. NEA is dedicated to creating harmonic environments and rich educational programs to guide youth to connect with cosmic intelligence and embody their divine nature and mastery as they build the New Earth.

Ron and I have dedicated our lives to supporting this Grand Transition. We stand alongside all of you as humanity awakens to its True Nature and becomes a People of Light in the heavenly reality of New Earth.

New Earth Ascending is dedicated to assisting people to realize their divinity and manifest that truth in every aspect of their life. For more information about New Earth Ascending or to contact Michael, please scan the QR code below for a list of resources and links, or visit *www.newearthascending.org*. Be sure to check out our courses including the Illuminated Quantum Healing practitioner course.

New Earth Ascending is a registered 508 (c)(1)(a) Self-Supported Non-profit Church Ministry with a global outreach. We greatly appreciate your support as we create new systems, communities, and schools for the development of the New Earth civilization. If you would like to make a tax-deductible donation to support our mission, please go to:

https://donorbox.org/donationtonewearthascending

Scan with a smart device camera for more information!

NEW EARTH ASCENDING
VISIONARY CREED

We acknowledge the sovereignty and equality of all levels of Creation and support the liberation of all of Life from cycles of suffering. We believe in the power of divine sovereign creatorship endowed to us by God/Source and dedicate our life to Light and Love in service to All. We believe in conscious participation, empowering everyone to activate awakening in themselves and their community.

We recognize free will and surrender our will and desires to the higher will of the Divine. We believe in divine timing and practice trust, patience, and tolerance as we witness the unfoldment of the perfection of the Divine Plan. We believe in the potency of empowering prayer, meditation, and ritual as tools for communication with the Divine for the culmination of spiritual light and divine wisdom. We believe everyone has a direct connection to the Source and no intermediary is needed. When we come together in fellowship, prayer, and devotion, we amplify the light of each individuals' loving intention through our unified, heart-centered consciousness.

We seek to uplift all groups and communities so that we may celebrate our unity, diversity, and wholeness. New Earth Ascending is non-competitive and embraces an ecumenical relationship with all religions and wisdom traditions. We believe in interfaith and inter-spirituality, acknowledging the teachings of Light, Love, and Wisdom in many traditions, philosophies, and cultures. We believe that no single religion holds the keys to the Kingdom of God and the blessings of redemption are available to all people through their unbreakable innate connection to the Godhead.

We believe in the Law of Oneness and that all of Creation emanates from one Divine Source that has both masculine and feminine principles. As we heal and balance the divine masculine and divine feminine principles within us, we embody the divine androgyny of Source and Nature as a harmonic synthesis of Spirit and Matter.

We believe that humanity and planet Earth are going through a rapid physical and spiritual transformation called by many as The Ascension or The Event. We believe this process to be part of a higher evolutionary divine plan guided by the Source of Creation and legions of beings working for the Light. This evolutionary process is multidimensional and is beyond the standard biological evolution spoken of by modern science.

We believe that we, as humanity, are awakening to our spiritual Self and are becoming a heart-based, unity-focused species with higher, multidimensional awareness, which some call Christ Consciousness, Cosmic Consciousness, or 5D Consciousness. We believe this transformation's power is happening through our divinely designed and curated DNA as the physical body transforms into a less dense body of Light with tremendously expanded multidimensional abilities.

We believe that Planet Earth, the sentient being of Gaia, is going through a similar restoration process and will soon transform into a revitalized higher dimensional planet, which many are calling the New Earth. Earth changes, weather events, crumbling institutional structures, frequency fluctuations, and astrological phenomena are all signs that we are nearing that shift into the next Golden Age, where Heaven and Earth become one and all systems of control and limitation will fall away.

We believe that we are supported by benevolent higher dimensional, subterranean, and extraterrestrial beings that work in harmonic collaboration with the higher evolutionary Divine Plan of Source. We believe that soon humanity will be consciously reunited with these benevolent beings and serve the higher evolutionary plan of the Light and Love of Source as cosmic co-citizens of the Multiverse working as one Family of Light in service to all of Creation.

We understand that the pathway of Self/Source-Realization and Ascension is comprised of self-study, self-practice, self-discipline, and steadfastness. We practice self-care and self-purification to clarify our Light. We acknowledge and value the acceleration of this process when we practice together in groupings of two or more in fellowship and worship.

We strive to grow in awareness and focused attention, practicing mindfulness in all areas of our lives to grow as conscious, heart-centered creators. We choose to focus our life positively with faith and knowing that Life is evolving in perfection following the Divine Plan of the Supreme Source.

We believe in the power of intention. We practice nonviolence and non-harmfulness in intention, thought, and action. We strive to release all forms of judgment and dual thinking. We honor the sacred heart's radiant potential and believe loving compassion and understanding to be The Way. We practice the heart-centered qualities of gentleness, reverence, loving-kindness, and forgiveness as pathways to reconciliation to emulate the eternal grace of Source and our Earth Mother, Gaia.

We see that Truth is alive within each of us, and we practice inner reflection to grow in discernment for what energies are resonant with our inner Source and our path. We practice benevolent truthfulness, honesty, straightforwardness, and vulnerability to embody and vocalize our deepest truth.

We value and practice transparency and accountability, believing in the opportunity for spiritual growth through spiritual partnership with our community members. We recognize one another as divine mirrors, reflecting to us where we are in our vibration, beliefs, and intentions.

We practice sacred sexuality as an alchemical tool for Divine Union and Ascension. We strive to purify our intentions and desires to align with Higher Love and authentic connection. We believe in heart-based self and consensual mutual pleasure to unite body, mind, and spirit so that we may deepen in our love and authentic connection to our Divine Self, our partner(s), and Creation.

We practice contentment, acceptance, appreciation, and gratitude for our life's many blessings and lessons. We practice non-attachment, non-possessiveness, non-stealing, non-excess, and sustainability, for all we need is given to us through our alignment with our Creator Source and our connection to our Earth Mother. We practice stewardship and sustainable selfless service, acknowledging our responsibility to take care of the world around us and within.

We practice sacred commerce, investing our resources, time, and energy towards the greater good and sustainability of our community and planet. We believe in reciprocal energy exchange and strive to do so when able. We practice generosity, hospitality, and charitability as reflections of the abundance of the Universe.

We strive to embody and emulate these spiritual principles to manifest the complete liberation of all beings from cycles of suffering and to assist this Grand Transition into the New Earth.

Bless us all!

GATEWAY FIVE: LAYING OF HANDS

Reiki & Beyond

This section instructs the reader in the healing art of the laying of hands. Instruction is given for personal healing, sharing healing energy with others, and working together in a group to channel spiritual Light.

ONE

High Alchemy of the Soul

Alchemy is the practice of transforming energy from one form to another. Alchemy is commonly understood in stories of turning water into wine or simple metal into gold. High Alchemy, the alchemy of the soul, is the transformation from mundane consciousness to the discovery and embodiment of one's True Divine Nature. This process activates and accelerates as the Mysteries of Creation and Laws of the Universe begin to be revealed to the honest seeker of Higher Knowledge and Wisdom of the Divine.

All alchemical processes need a container for transformation. The alchemical container for high alchemy is mindful awareness. Mindfulness is the practice of bringing our life's gross and subtle manifestations into the light of our awareness. Nondual awareness is the ability to see beyond the illusion of duality and see with the eyes of loving awareness. The spiritual alchemist uses mindfulness to observe limiting beliefs and patterns to refine distortions and misperceptions with compassionate understanding and spiritual knowledge.

Divine Embodiment

As we awaken and transform our worldly conditionings and limited thinking, we begin to embody the Light of our Divine Nature. Divine embodiment is a process of spiritual evolution where we give form through our beingness to higher spiritual virtues and anchor the Light of our True Nature into our human form. Every moment we can use self-inquiry and self-reflection to understand the origin of our thoughts and actions and what fuels our intentions in life. From this vantage point, we can discern which intentions, words, and actions are a reflection of our pure consciousness and which impulses come from our unprocessed trauma and worldly conditionings.

Manifestation

Manifestation is the process of bringing nonphysical energy into physical creation. Our life circumstances are a manifestation of inner experience and the intentions we carry, many of which are buried in our subconscious mind. As we awaken, we reclaim our powers of Divine Creatorship and become deliberate creators. As we take our power back from our subconscious limiting beliefs, we begin to attract higher manifestations at increasing speeds.

The magic behind manifestation is vibration. When our dominant vibration is high, our mind is fortified by love and higher truth and we attract more of what we want and experience synchronous events as we begin to see how the matrix of Creation works. When our vibration is low and our mind is infiltrated by distorted perception, we experience little to no synchronicity and attract manifestations that reflect those limiting beliefs and unprocessed traumas which create our inner distortion.

Our intention, our inner resolve, drives and motivates our path of creation. As we start on our awakening path, we become aware of our inner experience and refine our beingness into its highest golden nature and expression. We begin to manifest higher and higher creations and draw forth our own version of Heaven on Earth.

The Journey of a Thousand Miles Begins with One Step

The hero's journey is a framework of spiritual evolution found in many stories of beings who have pushed the upper limits of their consciousness and abilities to reach a higher state of exaltation and freedom. This is a path of initiation where a being departs the old ways to pursue higher knowledge, wisdom, and experience.

The hero or heroine's journey consists of three stages:

1. The Departure where the initiate leaves the known world and crosses the threshold into the unknown.

2. The Initiation phase is where the initiate must face challenges and grow into a higher version of themselves.

3. The Return phase is where the initiate, having been transformed into a new expression of themselves, brings the mystical elixir, the wisdom of their experience, back home to be used as a force of healing and transformation for the good of all. Let us look more closely at each phase to understand the mystical journey a bit deeper.

Departure: The Call to Adventure

All quests begin with a call to adventure, an inner yearning to journey beyond the horizons of what is currently thought or experienced and be initiated into higher awareness and understanding. It takes surrender and trust to follow the initiate's path and truly "Know Thyself." To choose awakening means to release attachment to all you have known and identified as. It takes nothing short of bravery to awaken.

Many hear the call and are afraid to leave the mundane behind, hoping to snooze for "just five more minutes." This is likely due to fear, a sense of duty or obligation, insecurity, or any other limiting or self-sabotaging beliefs that keep people from taking a leap of faith into uncharted territory. Some people will live in perpetual states of suffering for long periods of time because they do not believe they are capable or worthy of the change and growth they desire. Awakening is a choice that is constantly asking to be renewed as we become increasingly more aware of our inner realm, actions, and the repercussions of those actions on our life.

Awakening means taking full ownership of the circumstances of our life. Many would rather stay in a victim mentality of negatively polarized consciousness than accept that their life circumstances have been chosen and created by them, mostly unconsciously, for the purpose of spiritual growth. Many would rather stay in their story of suffering and "play it small" than take brave steps to make new choices and face the void of the unknown. Many hear the call, but only the brave embark on such a mysterious journey of high alchemy.

An Honest Prayer

On some level, the consciousness of the individual petitions the Godhead/Universe/Light/Spirit to show them the truth, and they send out an honest prayer or plea from the heart. This reaching for something higher is a crucial step in the initiation process. This prayer comes when one has experienced enough of the issues that have manifested from protecting the ego and personality. All the ways of "going it alone" have become exhausted. Often the emotions have become so painful that a person humbles themself and calls out from their heart to be shown the Truth, to be shown The Way.

From here, Spirit begins to work with the consciousness of the being to mature it to a sovereign, divine embodiment.

Supernatural Aid

Once the adventurer decides to accept the call to journey into the unknown, a seemingly serendipitous event occurs where a guide, physical or nonphysical, appears to point the initiate towards the higher path. Maybe it is someone who has information or resources that point to more wisdom and keys to unlock the mysteries. Maybe it is a dream or vision that activates the person and encourages them to seek out more information. Maybe it is a series of signs and synchronicities that are hard to ignore. I highly recommend watching the movie, *The Matrix*, which has many keys for awakening. The supernatural aid in this movie is when Neo, the main character who questions the nature of reality, receives a message that the Matrix is real and is invited to a meeting where he can learn about the truth of the reality matrix he is trapped in.

Threshold Guardians

The Threshold Guardians are the forces that attempt to keep the adventurer from following their path. Maybe this shows as relationships that try to control you or sow seeds of doubt, shame, guilt, or fear for desiring to expand beyond what is currently known, accepted, and experienced. Maybe it is the journeyer's limiting, self-sabotaging belief structures that keep them from taking the step towards a new way of life. These are just obstacles on the path of mastery and the initiate must truly trust their path and intuition and believe they are worthy of receiving the benefits that growth brings. If they succumb to the inner shadow or the pressures of the outer world, they will inherently experience more limitation and suffering until they follow the call. Once they affirm that they are ready and forge onward on the path less traveled, the magic of transformation can truly begin.

Initiation: Crossing the Threshold

Every person has a unique story to share about how they began to awaken. Every one of them is beautiful and powerful in its own way. Maybe it was gradual, maybe it was sudden. Maybe it was gentle, or maybe it was traumatic. Maybe it was practical. Maybe it was mystical. Everyone who begins to awaken has some initiation experience that points them towards a higher destiny pathway and a higher consciousness reality. These events, people, and experiences activate within them the desire to "know thyself." Slowly, the layers of misidentification peel away as they begin to deprogram their consciousness and ascend out of the limited cultural programming, ancestral trauma, and personal identifications, aversions, desires, fears, and attachments.

When one decides to seek the Mysteries and higher consciousness and steps beyond the default paradigm, they will be tested to measure their commitment to their sovereignty and awakening path. Some people may be threatened by new ideas and unusual behavior and try to lure the new traveler back into the old world, their old character, and limited egoic identification. This is just a test for the initiate, an opportunity to trust their inner guidance and inner knowing and take action towards their higher ideal expression and true liberation.

Trusting one's inner voice of wisdom and reason is the foundation for the path of spiritual growth. Awakening involves honoring the inner voice of Spirit and releasing habits that give our power away to outside authority. Heaven/God is within each of us, softly guiding us towards everything we have ever wanted. We are always being presented with the same option: acknowledge and follow the presence and guidance of the divine felt within or follow "The World" and outside authority. One leads us to salvation, the other keeps us in cycles of suffering and endless reincarnation cycles.

Mentorship: A Guide to Show the Way

As we begin to awaken, we start to look, consciously or unconsciously, for a teacher or mentor to guide us to higher truth. All good teachers, true teachers, point us back to the power we have within our beingness, to the "teacher that lives within." These mentors are role models for qualities that we want to mirror and embody. It is important to keep in mind that all beings are equal, and we risk disappointment when we put our teachers on pedestals. Many "spiritual teachers" on the Earth plane will reveal their own shadow as we move further along the ascension pathway. There are many teachers and spiritual leaders who use spiritual knowledge and their influence as a teacher to fulfill service-to-self agendas. Hidden agendas are hard to hide in an increasingly telepathic and intuitive culture. All of us are subject to our humanness and all hidden agendas will eventually be brought into the light of awareness.

Once we have learned all that we can from one teacher, we move to the next teacher. We are meant to use many teachers in our life path, and we limit ourselves by devoting ourselves to one teacher or guru. In truth, everyone and every life circumstance is our teacher.

The message that we received through clients is that "They," the spiritual beings that tend to the development of Earth and humanity, have coordinated it so that there will no longer be one source of divine wisdom and prophecy on the planet because the "Savior" and "Guru" templates cause people to lower in vibration and give their power away. Instead, "They" are spreading the dissemination of spiritual information and insight across the globe through many people to keep a higher balance. Anyone or any group that says that they are the savior or that only they know the divine truth is likely using this to generate fear or manipulate people for their service-to-self agenda. The true teacher lives within, and no outside authority supersedes your innate connection to the Divine.

Initiations: Trials and Errors

Each relationship and life circumstance is a course in spiritual growth, an educational alchemical container for transformation. The coursework involves understanding our emotions' hidden meaning and bringing more awareness to our thoughts, habits, beliefs, and actions. As we move through a course, we experience certain conditions to stimulate the potential for spiritual growth, consciousness expansion through trials and tribulations, and the insight these experiences bring. Every moment is ripe with the potential for deeper awareness and spiritual growth as one begins to consciously transform into higher consciousness. If we do not learn the lesson, it comes back around again in another circumstance or another relationship.

Helpers along the Journey

At certain points in the initiation phase, helpers appear on our path to encourage our growth and expansion. Sometimes it is pleasant and sometimes the relationship is challenging. As we awaken, we start to see our relationships as catalysts for spiritual growth. We begin to grow in our awareness that what we judge or fear in another reflects our inner world. Many people leave one relationship, only to manifest and recreate the same circumstances in another relationship. When you are in a spiritual relationship with another, you see the other as an ally for spiritual growth. As we shed the victim mentality and take authority over our experience as Divine Creators, we see that the biggest villains in our life, especially the characters involved in the most painful experiences, served as powerful activators for massive healing and consciousness expansion. It is up to each of us to cultivate a compassionate heart so that we can tend to our wounds and realize the deeper teachings of our traumas.

Growth: New Skills

Each challenge in our life is an opportunity to grow spiritually. We can use alchemical practices to transform our stagnation, stored trauma, and limiting beliefs. We can read literature that inspires higher thought and understanding. The more we use our skills and acquired knowledge, the better our life becomes and the more automatic and integrated the new understanding becomes. Questions lead to more questions as we come to a deeper and deeper understanding of our True Self. True nourishment is that which feeds our soul and sets us free.

The Abyss: Ego Death & Spiritual Rebirth

The Dark Night of the Soul is a spiritual crisis period for an awakening initiate as their old identities and beliefs go through a death process. This is a deeply transformative phase as the light is seemingly stripped from the world. Deep churning, pain, doubt, fear, and grief often color the experience of this Dark Night. The Dark Night of the Soul finishes as the initiate discovers the light within them and begins to embody a higher expression of themself. Rising like the phoenix from the ashes, they emerge with deeper insight and wisdom. Miracles are simply a shift of perception from fear to higher love and unity. When we release our addictive thinking towards fear and discover the source of safety and abundance found within, we begin to access our power as divine creators and limitless beings.

Final Changes

Once we are finished with one course, we move into a higher-level course to achieve a better understanding. We see this outpictured in the changing of relationships, jobs, homes, and so on. Often, right before our "graduation," a final test, a final opportunity emerges to see if we are truly ready to move into the next level of consciousness exploration. We are meant to change and grow. Some people may have a difficult time accepting that you act differently or have new boundaries. While it may be uncomfortable, this is simply a test to see if you are truly committed to embodying your deepest truth or if there are still places in your consciousness where you get hooked into old patterns that need to be reconciled before you can be fully anchored in your new embodiment. It is in this phase that the initiate receives revelations that illuminate the mind to higher truths that liberate their consciousness and create a higher perspective of their life. Finally, the sword is pulled from the stone, and victory has been achieved! Now the victorious adventurer can begin their quest back home.

Atonement: Reconciliation

As we awaken, we may find that we have harmed someone else when we were caught in the illusion of our ego or a less enlightened state. It is important to make amends and reconcile with those we may have wronged. The best way to make amends is to transform your limiting beliefs and stored trauma that caused the suffering. From this place, you can approach the situation with the intention to relieve the suffering of others. Reconciliation involves healing the hearts of all parties involved and coming to a deeper understanding. To love others as we love ourselves effectively, we need to first love ourselves unconditionally. Grace is available for all, no matter how terrible the action is.

Ho'oponopono is a Hawaiian healing practice for reconciliation and forgiveness. It can be translated into four steps and phrases: "I am sorry, I love you, please forgive me, and thank you." When we say "I am sorry" to another, it shows that we have thought about our actions and see that we have potentially caused harm to another. We say "I love you" to let them know that we release the fight and want positive solutions for all involved. When we say "please forgive me," we invite them to be a part of the healing process. They may also want to confess their role in the issue. We say "thank you" because we have come to a deeper understanding of how this opportunity provided nourishment for our growth.

We do not need the other person to forgive us to release ourselves from feelings of guilt. That is our wound to heal. When we do our part of the work, we release our part of the karma with this person and can truly stand in sovereign support of the other's growth. We can do this process for loved ones far away and even those who have traveled beyond the physical world.

A Gift from the Universe

When we complete our missions, there is often a gift from the universe for persevering through challenges. Maybe it is a physical item, an opportunity to share your new skills or talents, or some other blessings of abundance from the universe. Facing your inner shadow is tough work! Being sure to thank God/the Universe for blessing you will open the pathways for even greater blessings!

Return Changed

"We only keep what we have by giving it away." is an adage from 12-step programs that perfectly describes the final stage in the cycle of the hero's journey. As we learn to make peace with our inner distortions and transform into the limitless nature of our Divine Self, we stand as emanations of Higher Understanding and Higher Love. We broadcast this frequency into the world through our very being. We then carry within our essence a healing elixir, wisdom that can be shared with those who seek a higher truth. It is our responsibility to humanity to share our spiritual insight and discovered gifts. Our heroic characters from humanity's history were pioneers, rebels, visionaries, and artists who pushed the upper limits of what was thought possible to achieve the seemingly impossible.

From their new heights, many have borrowed strength and inspiration to walk their own path of initiation. Each of us carries these extraordinary potentials within us. Each of us can be pioneers of consciousness that help to unshackle the collective of humanity by first taking the shackles off of our own self.

May these words shared here fuel your path of liberation, your own hero's journey, so that you can bring back the wisdom you have discovered within and share it as medicine for this world.

TWO

Reiki: Laying of Hands

Reiki Precepts:
Just for today, I will give thanks for my many blessings.
Just for today, I will not worry.
Just for today, I will not be angry.
Just for today, I will do my work honestly.
Just for today, I will be kind to my neighbor and every living thing.
—Dr. Mikao Usui

Many ancient cultures around the world have systems of healing that involve the laying of hands to clarify, heal, and balance body systems. As a child, I was fascinated by the stories of Jesus and the disciples healing people from illness and even resurrecting the dead. When I heard or read these stories, something moved within me as I fantasized about what it might be like to do something like this.

During my awakening process, I was introduced to the Usui System of Natural Healing, more commonly referred to as *Reiki*. This system gave me the foundational teachings of the laying of hands and channeling Divine Energy for healing. The dogma and limitations of how the method was taught by some teachers inspired me to continue searching for a Higher Truth regarding channeling and casting light (laying of hands). Contemporary use of the word "Reiki" has become synonymous with the laying of hands and spiritual light casting.

Since learning *Reiki*, I have studied other philosophies of hands-on healing from different perspectives. My ideas of what Reiki is have evolved beyond what is usually taught in traditional Western practices of Reiki. I have also learned much about hands-on healing through my clients during hypnosis sessions. I have merged all this information into a practice that I call Embodied Light, although these practices are inherently interwoven throughout all my teachings and offerings.

Embodied Light is a system of practices you can use to raise your personal vibration and guide you into your most radiant embodied expression. These practices are easy to learn, and anyone can use them. Embodied Light's system uses meditation techniques, breathing practices, healing touch, movement, and energy attunements to support you in feeling grounded, centered, and joyously free.

These practices, many of which are in this book, focus the intention of one's being on compassionate, heart-based living. All ancient traditions speak of the power of the heart and the importance of beliefs based on unconditional love and reverence for life. As we learn to concentrate on spiritual principles like forgiveness, gratitude, bravery, honesty, and unconditional love, we can manifest a world that reflects those same values.

Embodied Light training encourages the cultivation of individual spirituality and a personal relationship with the Divine Source. We honor the Light and Wisdom of all traditions and faith practices. These practices can create a new spiritual path for yourself or enhance the religious and spiritual practices you already study.

What is Reiki?

Reiki is made of two Japanese words *Rei* and *Ki*. *Rei* means "spiritual wisdom," and *ki* means energy.

The laying of hands works with what Dr. J.J. Hurtak, the writer of *The Keys of Enoch*, calls the Shekinah Universe, the inner universe that transforms Creation. The power of the laying of hands comes from the Shekinah, the Divine Presence/Holy Spirit which activates the spiritual gifts in humanity. It is what people call Reiki — the nurturing, regenerative Light force of the Divine.

When a practitioner lays hands on a client, or when a person "runs energy" for self-healing, I teach my students to intentionally connect to Source/God/Goddess and invite the Divine Energies to flow through them to use for healing. As the energy passes through the channel of the practitioner, it raises their vibration to match the higher frequency of energy that begins to flow through them from the Source.

This should put anyone's religious fears to sleep as the number one thing I hear from Christians is that they are forbidden to work with healers because it goes against Christ and God. This is understandable since the true teachings and life of Jesus have been heavily distorted. As you can see, practitioners of Reiki and the sacred teachings of the Judeo-Christian lineages are speaking of the same healing power.

Reiki is active prayer that brings the power of heaven into this world. Any religious figures that shame or condemn the use of these healing practices are heavily programmed and working within a control system that is not reflective of the Grace of God. I suggest for anyone in such a dogmatic religious group to discover the Truth of the Living Christ Within You who is beaming encouragement for you to use these tools for healing and awakening to your own Christhood.

Embodied Light Reiki Principles

Reiki is Non-Religious

Learning to cast light and be a lightworker will enhance any spiritual or religious practices. For many, learning to work with Divine Light is the first time they feel a true connection to God or Spirit. Learning to channel reiki is available to all people regardless of religious background.

Anyone Can Learn

Learning to work with Light and transmit Source-sent energy is simple to do, and anyone can learn it. It is our birthright. We are extensions of Source energy and extensions of Source's plan for creating harmony within the Universe.

Do All Healers Use Source Energy?

There are many forms of energy healing being practiced all around the world. Some people are taught to use their own energy for healing. Some pull energy from the world around them. Some use the energy of the Earth. There are limitless sources of subtle energy. I always teach my students to connect with Source and invite the highest, clearest, and brightest light available and appropriate for the client.

It is important to use your heart and Inner Being for discernment when choosing an energy healer or energy teacher. You want to choose someone who embodies unconditional love and health. Many people use spirituality as a cover for negatively polarized agendas. Trust your intuition and choose a healer or teacher that uplifts and honors you as an individual.

Divinely Guided Healing

Reiki channeled through a person with the intention of healing is intelligent in that a practitioner simply needs to empty the mind and allow the energy to flow through them. The energy goes where it is most needed in the body. While someone may lay their hands on a specific area of the body, the energy begins to flow throughout the recipient's entire energy field, treating the whole system.

Holistic Healing Method

This is a holistic healing system that works on the physical, mental, emotional, psychic, and spiritual aspects of one's being because Reiki works with the fundamental building blocks of Creation. The laying of hands draws forth the radiant wholeness on all layers of one's being.

Reiki heals the superficial manifestation of disease and works to balance the root cause of whatever is causing the suffering by encouraging the natural ability of the body to self-regulate and heal itself.

Clear the Channel

Those working on others' energy should have a clear mind, body, and energy field. While being in a heart-based focus, a person should also be clean of chemicals and intoxicants so that the energy is not contaminated as it passes through the body.

Sharing Divine Energies

Once one has dedicated their vessel and life to working for the Light and has received an activation through an attunement ceremony, self-attunement through prayer and intention, or spontaneous divine activation, all that is needed to run the energies is to lay the hands with the intention of healing. When this is done, a bridge is established consciously or unconsciously, and the energy begins to flow from Source through the practitioner's heart and overall energy field. All one needs to do is call on the

Light for healing and allow it to flow through you. This is your birthright!

Reiki/Source Energy Is Non-Harming

Reiki is non-harming and life-supporting. You can never give too much or too little. Although, recipients of the healing energy may not ever want you to stop! Source Intelligence is Love, and it restores everything it touches.

Channeling Source Energy Never Depletes Your Energy

It is important to understand that we are not using our personal energy to create healing when we work with reiki. Energy medicine practitioners who do this often feel depleted, and many develop illnesses or at the very least, burnout because they use their own energy for healing others. When we use reiki, we become a channel for the endless supply of Source energy. As reiki passes through us, it heals us. While it may be tiring at first to focus or stand for the duration of a healing session, most of the time, a practitioner feels charged and buzzed by the high energies they channel during a healing session.

Levels of Embodied Light Reiki

Level 1: Personal Healing and Lightbody Ascension

This level focuses on self-healing and the ascension process. We explore subtle energy basics and subtle energy anatomy. We focus on developing personal self-healing practices and setting a foundation for living a spiritually focused life.

Level 2: Reiki Practitioner

This level is about sharing reiki and energy medicine with others, in-person or remotely. Business training is offered for those who wish to use this work as part of their professional services.

Level 3: Reiki Master Teacher

During this level of training, initiates are taught how to initiate and teach others Reiki and energy medicine.

Attunement and Initiation

Divine Light is available to all people simply by having the intention to connect with the loving redemptive energy of Source and allowing the connection to flow. Through this intention, you connect to the truth of what you are, a conduit for Source energy.

Many souls have been doing this healing work in other lifetimes and find the process of channeling Light simple and natural. For others, working with a teacher is essential to activate or enhance this ability in through a powerful process called an attunement.

An attunement is an alchemical ceremony to connect a person to higher frequencies of Source energy to use for healing. The process enhances the recipient's natural ability to connect to divine Light and "opens the pipes" for more energy to stream through. While self-attunements are certainly possible and valid, being attuned and trained by a teacher proficient at working with these healing energies is often a life-changing experience that brings deep insight and healing to the recipient. Multiple attunement/initiation ceremonies can be done depending on the teacher's lineages or the needs of the student.

Self-Healing Tool: What Are You Ready to Understand and Heal?

The attunement ceremony is a powerful statement for the recipient. It is a declaration that they are dedicating their vessel to light for personal and global healing. As they welcome these healing energies into their being, a powerful process begins as lower energies and blockages begin to be cleared from the body of the initiate. The entire cellular structure begins to shift as Source energy begins to transform the DNA to hold a higher frequency of Source light. Over the next few weeks, many people experience physical, emotional, and spiritual changes as the system begins to heal and raise in frequency. It is recommended to practice daily self-healing to support the integration process.

Manifestation Tool: What Are You Calling into Your Life?

The attunement process is also a powerful technology for manifestation. I ask my students to set an intention of what they want to call into their life experience. During the attunement and the weeks following, their frequency rises to meet their desired outcome and draws it to them.

In-Person or Distance Attunements

There is a great benefit in receiving multiple attunements throughout one's lifetime. Each attunement helps to clear out stagnant energy and blockages so that one can become a more powerful and clear channel for reiki. These transformative ceremonies can be done in person or guided from a long distance as we are all connected through the Unified Field of Creation.

Once I "uploaded" an attunement for a friend with the intention for her to receive the attunement at a specific time. My friend could not "tune in" during that time, and it took her a few days to do so. As she laid down to connect, her heart rate began to increase as healing energies began to course through her body. She was wearing a device that measured her heart rate throughout the day. When she checked the measurements to see what her heart rate was during the meditation where she received the attunement, she noticed it was higher than when she had been on a rigorous hike earlier that day. At the time, I was still struggling with the dogma taught by the Usui Reiki system I had been trained in that insisted attunements are only valid and effective in person. This experience was all I needed to shatter that belief and align with the higher truth of limitless Source energy.

Various Experiences

Each initiation ceremony is unique to each person. Like my own first attunement, some people hardly experience anything significant but have a feeling that they participated in something deeply meaningful as they committed themselves to healing and working with light.

Other times, people may experience flowing energies and various sensations as their body systems restructure to become a clearer vessel and channel for Source energy. People may see colors in their meditative state or are reconnected with spirit guides, star families, or loved ones who have passed on. Some people experience spontaneous healing as they shed old energies no longer needing manifested symptoms to teach them a lesson. Every experience, subtle or profound, is exactly what the recipient needs on their individual path of awakening and healing.

Integration after Attunement

Over the next few weeks, some people may experience healing symptoms like headaches, tiredness, and other indications that the body is releasing toxins and old energies as it moves through a process of healing. Doing self-treatments can reduce discomfort and speed up the healing process as the body aligns with the new energies.

Power of Three: A Holy Trinity for Healing

A channel needs to understand that they are not solely responsible for creating a healing experience. For healing to happen, the channel, recipient, and Source need to be in equal agreement with what level of healing is appropriate and possible. If there is resistance within any member of the trinity, the healing will only go so far. Let's look at this from the perspective of each part of the triad.

One: Source and the Soul of a Client

A client may have agreed to experience these conditions to balance karma or create conditions for others' learning on a soul level. If complete healing is not aligned with their soul path, in agreement with the Divine Plan for that soul, it will not happen no matter how many sessions they have. In instances like this, it is important that the practitioner does not take this as a personal reflection of their abilities but instead, surrenders to the Higher Will and Divine Plan. The client can continue to meditate and adapt their perspectives and behaviors to truly discover the true source of their suffering. Many times in my sessions, the Higher Self will not do complete healing because the client needs to work on themselves for it to create the transformation they desire.

Two: Client/Recipient

To heal completely, a recipient needs to be willing to release the old energies, identifications, and belief systems that keep them in a cycle of dis-ease/disease and discomfort. This requires self-reflection, honesty, and a commitment to embodying higher truth. Illness and stress are invitations for self-awareness and deeper understanding. Some people are not ready to take those steps. People often create an identity for themselves through their suffering. Therefore, a good intake conversation is crucial to see where a client is open to change.

Three: Practitioner

It is our noble responsibility to hold the highest vision for our clients. An effective practitioner of any transformative therapy puts aside judgments and embodies their Higher Self, who only wants the best for the client. We surrender our will to the Divine's will and trust that whatever happens during the session was for the highest and best of all involved.

Intention, Attention, Compassion

All powerful energy healing sessions are conducted through the compassion of a heart of service guided by the Will and Love of Source. We become a channel for and presence of divine healing energies when we intend to connect and shine this healing energy. As we focus on the object we are wishing to transform, we bring the perfection that already exists forward into reality.

During the healing session, the channel is to remain focused on the intention of healing and service. If the practitioner is not able to hold the intention of running healing energy, the bridge disintegrates. Conscious breathing, visualization, and heart-centered focus are key elements to running Source energy for healing.

Consent

In honor of everyone's free will and power of Divine Creatorship, we need to ask permission to touch or send healing energies to others. When a person agrees to receive, their energy field opens to make way for the transmission. If a person is closed to receiving, it will likely cause more discomfort and suffering to attempt to lay hands. There are many stories, often of men, who use the disguise of a healing session to inappropriately touch another person. If something does not feel right about a healing session or the practitioner's vibe, you have every right to say something and reject the healing session.

Everyone has different parts of their body that they consider private. It is important to describe to a recipient where and how you will be applying light touch to their body and confirm that you have permission to do so. This is especially important for people who have never had hands-on healing work. This helps them relax their nervous system and open their bodies to receive healing.

If you are doing distant healing work, ask the recipient if they are open to receiving healing from afar. This agreement creates an energetic link for the exchange of energy. You may even want to synchronize times for them to tune in with you in some way, although this is not necessary.

If you cannot communicate with the person, you can intend to connect with the receiver's Higher Self through your own heart and see if the client is open to receiving. Trust the intuitive messages you receive in response. If you get a "no" or feel your own energy close, use your time for something else. If you get a "yes" or your energy "lights up," have fun connecting with this person for healing. If you get a "no" and feel that they may be open to this energy later, you can create a "bank" of healing energy that is available for them to receive when they *are* ready.

Using Symbols in a Healing Session

Symbols are a powerful way to activate and amplify intentions. Like the Usui Reiki symbols, many symbols are purely charged with the love of countless beings who have used them for healing. Using symbols that generate loving energy like rose petals, luminous hearts, and angels brings those symbols' energies into the sessions. Some people use Light language codes (divinely imbued symbols) that they receive through their Higher Self and guides to adjust the frequency of the Light they channel to create a variety of healing effects.

Symbols are a wonderful tool to train our ability to "turn the dial" on the energies. I always had resistance to the idea that a symbol "gives you power." If anything, your focus on the intention behind the symbol brings those qualities and intentions into your experience from your Inner Being. For some, learning the symbols is crucial to help them focus their intention and attention. For others, the symbols are a distraction and seem to limit. Follow your heart. It always knows best.

In the Usui System of Natural Healing, there are three symbols used for conducting healing sessions for people initiated into the second level of Reiki. Other symbols are used in the Master Level training and other forms of Reiki.

The first two symbols of the Usui System of Natural Healing are ancient Tibetan healing symbols. The third symbol is a Japanese *kanji*. These symbols are activated when you intend to use them. You can also draw them with the palm of your hand, visualize them, or chant their names to focus your intention and attention on the symbols' qualities. Reiki is limitless, and so are the uses for the symbols.

Out of respect for the lineages of Reiki, I have decided not to include the actual symbols in the book to protect and honor the sacredness of the lineages. They are shared in the Embodied Light course, or any Reiki master can share them with you after an attunement.

The Power Symbol: Cho Ku Rei — CKR

The Power Symbol amplifies the power of reiki. It can be used anywhere where you want to increase the healing energies. It can also be used to seal energy work. This is a wonderful symbol to use when charging objects like crystals or pendulums. Different people draw the symbol with different directions of the spiral. The way I was taught, start drawing the symbol from right to left with a clockwise spiral.

The Emotional/Mental Healing Symbol: Sei Hei Ki — SHK

The Emotional/Mental Healing symbol is used to transform emotional and mental patterns. This is a wonderful symbol to use when working with trauma and addictive patterns and to bring deeper clarity. Both CKR and SHK can be used to create healing spaces by placing the symbols on the walls of the space through visualization and intention.

Remote Viewing and the Distance Symbol: Hon Sha Ze Sho Nen — HSZSN

Remote viewing allows our mind to connect with the unified field of Creation to tune our conscious awareness into other aspects of Creation. We have local and nonlocal consciousness, meaning, we can be present and focused on our body, *and* we can also project our consciousness across space and time to remote view other people, places, realms, and time periods. We are not limited to one place and time. We simply need to calm our mind, set the intention to connect with the object of our focus, and listen to what is being communicated. From that shared connection, we can transmit and receive imagery, intentions, and healing energies.

The Distance Symbol is used for remote healing or when we want to beam Reiki over longer distances. It is also used to send healing energy into the past or into the future to be accessed later. To use this symbol for remote healing, simply draw, visualize, or chant the name of the symbol and dedicate the session to the recipient by stating their name or visualizing the person to which you are sending the healing energies. The same process is used if you were to send healing to another location on the planet.

In the Usui lineages, there are a few versions of this symbol since Hawayo Takata, protégé of Mikao Usui, shared different versions of the symbol with different students. It intends to connect to the timeless space of the unified field to transmit healing to the most appropriate place that is important here. That is the power of this symbol.

There is no limit to how we can work with the Light. We are only limited by our conditioned thinking. Be playful and allow your imagination and the power of your Inner Being to guide you into new and exciting ways to work with Light and Consciousness.

THREE

Pillars of Embodied Light Reiki

The process of conducting a hands-on healing session for yourself or another person is a simple structure that can create profound effects. The structure of a healing session can be organized into five pillars or sections.

Pillar One: Gassho Activation — Grounding, Centering, and Tuning In

From a seated position, bring your hands to your knees, palms down, and close your eyes, practicing conscious breathing as you tune into your subtle energy and inner realm. Connect with your hara line. As you inhale, lengthen your spine; as you exhale, ground your energy and soften any tension in your body. The same process can also be adapted to a standing posture with the hands gently touching the hara and the heart or any position that feels grounding.

Bring your hands to prayer at the heart center. In Japanese, this is called *Gassho*. In the Sanskrit traditions, this is called *Anjali Mudra*. In English, we simply call this Prayer Hands. Call upon the presence of the Light and feel your vibration begin to rise. Intend to activate the light of your heart, breathe into it, and expand this light. Feel the energy flow into your arms and activate the hands' minor chakras, the center of the palms, with the light of your heart. You may even want to rub the palms of the hands together to activate the electromagnetic fields of the hands.

We create a sacred temple of Light during this phase by bringing the Light into the healing space. Use your intention and attention to expand and clear your auric field to totally envelop the space you are working in. Invite your heart field to shine brightly!

Pillar Two: Reiji-ho Connection — Higher Mind, Guides, Client

This is the invitation where we invite the co-creators for the healing into our quantum healing space. You may feel the vibration raise or have other psychic experiences as higher beings' consciousness emerge within the quantum healing field. Trust your sensations.

Bring your prayer hands up to touch your thumbs on your forehead. Tune into the center of your skull and activate the Brow Center by intending for it to light up. Breathe into and expand this Light. Intend to activate your inner sight and your connection to the Higher Mind of Source and your Higher Self and guides. If you are working on another person, you can invite their higher consciousness and guides to work with your consciousness to guide you throughout the session.

Pillar Three: Chiryo Laying of Hands — Intuitive Session

The third pillar is the transmission of the healing energies. This is done through the laying of hands or psychically for remote sessions. Different traditions teach these steps differently. What is important is that you find a way that feels comfortable for you.

Hand Placements

When we work with our hands, we can learn a set pattern of hand positions to use or else allow the hand placements to be guided intuitively. While learning, set hand placements create a nice structure to ensure that the whole system is treated. Most practitioners find that a hands-on-healing session is an intuitive dance. I recommend practicing many different approaches to find your own unique way of feeling authentically connected and confident.

Sacred Touch: Listen, Feel, Trust

The electromagnetic field of the body extends many feet beyond the physical body. There are times that you may find your hands resting completely on the body, and other times, you may be guided to work with parts of the field that are further away from the surface. Trust your internal messages and sensations.

Let the hands hover close enough or far enough away from the physical body that you can sense the electric and magnetic qualities of the subtle energies being exchanged between your palms and the field that you are working on.

A lot of information is being exchanged the moment we intend to make the connection. Trust your sensations and inner messages. It takes a good minute or two to truly establish a deep connection. Some new students move around a lot when they first begin doing sessions. "Park it" for a little bit at each place you are guided to and simply listen to understand what is needed. Most of the time, a simple presence is enough to heal.

As we lay hands, we hold a high vibration within our entire field that "invites" the lower energies that we treat to raise in vibration. All kinds of events may happen as the energy shifts, including tingling sensations, hot/cold feelings, bodily noises, deep sighs of relief, shaking, and even strong emotional releases that include crying or screaming.

Whatever emerges, let it. Hold space for the energy to rise up to the surface to be felt and released. If someone is crying, do not stop them from crying. Allow it to continue for as long as needed. For many, fear of being alone has subconsciously blocked them from facing certain aspects of their life fully, and it is our job to hold a loving presence so that the energy can be integrated and released completely. If it continues for a few minutes, ask the client if they are okay. Most of the time, they will nod yes. I allow the crying to continue and direct more Light to the heart of the recipient.

Receiving Images and Intuitive Messages

While laying your hands on a client, pay attention to internal sensations, images, and messages. Nonphysical guidance comes in various forms and is different for everyone. Many start to rapidly develop psychic gifts and extrasensory abilities when they begin facilitating healing sessions. This may include mediumship, channeling, timeline work, and more. Trust what you receive. Release doubts that may arise after receiving intuitive guidance and stay in the flow.

Pillar Four: Closing and Sealing Sealing with Gratitude

Thank the Guides and Families of Light using *Reiji-Ho*. Bring your hands to *Reiji-ho*, hands in prayer position with thumbs touching the Brow Center. Take a moment to send gratitude to Source for this experience. Thank your spiritual allies for guiding and supporting the work. If you are working with another client, thank their guides and Higher Self as well. Tune in and listen if there are any final messages for you or the client. Messages from the Light will always be loving. Trust what you receive.

Dedicating Your Practice (Gassho)

Dedicate the fruits and efforts of your practice towards anything that you choose. A simple, yet powerful gesture is dedicating the practice towards the liberation of all beings from cycles of suffering.

Pillar Five: Disconnecting Energy Dry Bathing (Kenyo-ku)

This practice is helpful anytime you feel that you have "picked up" unwanted or extra energy from other people or places. There are many ways to do this, all of them have to deal with the intention of clearing any unwanted energy you may have picked up and returning to your own sovereign alignment, fully disconnected from the client/recipient.

Set the intention to stop the flow of energy from the hands to keep them from "running hot" all day, which is uncomfortable for some people and may create a "spacey" quality if left running all day. If you find your hands filling with energy throughout the day, use the energy for personal healing, healing the Earth, or even a pet. The energy is charging in the hands because something in the environment is in need. Go ahead and share!

I generally use *Kenyo-ku*, followed by washing my hands in cold water and splashing cool water on my face to reset the energy.

Kenyo-ku Dry Bathing

Set the intention to clear your energy and sever connections that no longer serve you.

Bring the right hand to the left shoulder, sweep the palm down and across your torso, brushing the end of the energy behind the right side of your hip. Repeat with the left hand. Repeat with the right.

Bring the right hand to the top of the left shoulder. Extend the left arm, palm facing upward. Swipe down the left arm with the left hand, brushing the energy off the left hand's fingertips. Repeat with the left hand sweeping the right arm. Repeat with the right hand sweeping the left arm.

Slide and clap your hands together as if you were brushing off dust. Do this three times with the intention of stopping the flow of energy from the hands.

Bring the hands to Gassho/Prayer Hands. Close your eyes to tune into your own energy field. Ground and center yourself. Bring your field in closer to your body and seal it with gratitude.

Distance and Self-Healing Time

After you facilitate a healing session for someone else, you are primed and ready to do self-healing or remote healing for others or the planet.

Take advantage of the "extra charge" and use it for something else if you have the time to do so. More instruction on Distance/Nonlocal healing is given in the Embodied Light appendix in the back of the book.

FOUR

Spiritual Ethics

The Eightfold Path of Buddhism offers us a set of ethical observances to help us grow in nobility. The practice of these observances is an ongoing reflection fueled by personal revelations. They help us to live a peaceful and orderly existence in the community. Practicing these values and virtues keeps us from creating more negative karma or from adding to the suffering of the world. These values meet the practitioner where they are on their path of awakening. Every life experience is valuable as we learn to discern what is essential for life and what distracts us from and distorts our vision of our True Nature.

The Eightfold Path of Buddhism is a guide to spiritual awakening and liberation from cycles of suffering. This path consists of moral conduct, mental discipline, and the attainment of divine wisdom. The word "samma," a Pali word, is often translated as "right." When used in this context, right is not describing a system of "right" and "wrong," but quality of expression rooted in compassion and illuminated by Higher Wisdom. As we learn to walk the path of righteous nobility guided by a loving heart, we embody the potential of the liberation of all beings from the cycles of suffering.

The root quality of these morals is *ahimsa*, nonviolence, and non-harming. We can look at our life or our consciousness as a garden. In our garden, we have many varieties of seeds planted. Some seeds are seeds of suffering. Some of these seeds are of compassion and love. In every moment, we have a choice to water our seeds of suffering or water our seeds of love and compassion. Living a righteous and noble life is a practice of watering the seeds of compassion and love. Make your garden beautiful by watering seeds of patience, tenderness, kindness, gentleness, and other qualities of love and compassion.

One: Right Understanding, Right View (Samma Ditthi)

The Four Noble Truths and the Three Characteristics of Existence can help us to better understand the nature of reality. We understand that how we see our self is always shifting and changing and that life is impermanent. We understand that suffering is inherent in life and that pleasurable moments eventually shift to less pleasurable moments. We understand we suffer because we hold conditioning from this world. We understand that not only does suffering occur but there is also a path to suffering. We understand liberation is possible and that there is a pathway to liberation.

Two: Right Intent, Right Resolve (Samma Sankappa)

This is our commitment to the path of awakening and dedication towards the liberation of all beings from suffering. This happens by guiding one's thoughts and intentions back to Unconditional Love and Oneness and dedicating our beingness to Service to All.

Three: Right Speech (Samma Vaca)

We can use our communication to relieve suffering and create harmonic agreements. This includes refraining from lying, using divisive or abusive speech, slander, and even idle gossip. Often people use communication to distract themselves from fully experiencing their Inner Being. Gandhi said, "Speak only if it improves upon the silence." Before communicating, ask yourself, "Is it kind? Is it true? Is it necessary? Is it helpful?"

Four: Right Action (Samma Kammanta)

With right action, we dedicate all actions of the body towards compassionate living and to relieving the suffering of all sentient beings. This includes nonviolence, non-stealing, and sacred sexuality.

Five: Right Livelihood (Samma Ajiva)

Our livelihood, our way of generating income, gathering resources, and creating a career path should be done honestly and in a way that promotes equality among all sentient life. This means that our work does not harm other beings or nature and that our participation in society reflects our Service to the Greater Good of Life.

Six: Right Effort (Samma Vayama)

We strive to train the mind towards wholesome, positive thoughts that create positive, life-affirming action. We grow in an "attitude of gratitude," shedding negative thoughts and making a conscious effort to move towards joyful determination.

Seven: Right Mindfulness (Samma Sati)

We practice training the mind and our conscious awareness to be fully focused on the present moment. This includes growing in our awareness of the body, feelings, mind, thoughts, breath, and the ever-shifting phenomenon that we call reality.

Eight: Right Concentration (Samma Samadhi)

This is the practice of joining the mind with the Absolute. Seeing Heaven on Earth through single-pointed meditation, which results in unbroken attentiveness and a deep feeling of tranquility and bliss.

Creating Pathways of Transformation

While each of us has different karma, different mental patterning, and different soul contracts, there are simple key principles that can be applied to any negative condition to transform it into a higher state. If we wish to purify our bodymind complex, we need to follow fours steps:

1. Cease to deny the presence of patterns within our mind that cause suffering for ourselves and others.
2. Cease justification of those patterns.
3. Release guilt around the patterns of distortion and limitation that we carry.
4. Actively seek out and practice methods of purification and God/Self-realization.

Mental Alchemy: Evolving to Higher Thought

The mind is constantly generating thoughts. Some are pleasant and empowering, and others are generated from the shadows of our unprocessed trauma and ignorance. When one becomes aware of negative thoughts that keep us in cycles of suffering, we have three options to make change.

1. Discard the thought, jerk it out of the mind.
2. Discard the thought for a higher vibrational thought. ("I bind this thought pattern of anger. I call forth and set loose the power of serenity.)
3. Intensify the thought/emotion and direct it towards Source such as in the tantric traditions. This option should be done with caution as intensifying powerful negative emotion/desire/thought can cause more chaos and suffering.

Seven Pillars of Personal Transformation)

Below are seven keys for personal transformation to guide you through your awakening and ascension processes. Use each key to fine-tune your actions to create lasting positive change.

One: Sankalpa — Intention

Intention is everything on the path of awakening. *Sankalpa* is an intention that comes from the heart and serves your Higher Path. Sometimes we have unconscious intentions of avoiding suffering or discomfort, which keep us from going through the experiences that give valuable insight into the nature of our suffering. This concept is reflected in Newton's First Law of Motion which states that an object will remain at rest or motion until acted upon by another force. Your intention is the force that creates the architecture and trajectory of your future.

Attention and *intention* are qualities of consciousness. *Attention* energizes consciousness. Wherever the mind goes, the energy follows, and we become increasingly aware of what we focus upon. *Intention* transforms whatever we hold within the container of our awareness.

Intention shapes our destiny. Unconscious intentions are those of our subconscious and often operate in the background. Most of humanity operates with the unconscious intention to survive and protect their body and future. They haphazardly fumble through life from one event to another, from one emotional reaction to another, asleep in their own dream.

As we awaken and begin to become deliberate conscious creators of our reality, we begin to focus our intention and attention in a way that sustains us on our path of spiritual growth and personal mastery.

Two: Tapas — Intensity and Dedication

This is related to Newton's Second Law of Motion, which states, "The rate of change of momentum of a body with respect to time is directly proportional to the net external force acting on the body." Spiritual growth is dependent on the intensity and duration of our practice. Our commitment can be seen as low, medium, or high intensity.

Three: Shani — Slowing

Becoming aware of our subconscious drives requires us to slow down our physical, mental, and emotional actions to understand the subtle and nuanced shifts in our consciousness. While high-intensity practices may result in faster spiritual growth, it is important to discern when rest and a gentler pace are what is most needed.

Four: Vidya — Deep Awareness, Clear Sight

Self-inquiry and mindfulness help us see and understand our habits and self-limiting, self-sabotaging patterns to transform them into higher states. Mindfulness of any condition immediately begins to transform the condition into a higher state through loving awareness.

Five: Abhaya — Fearlessness, Bravery

Change takes courage. Lasting change requires us to acknowledge our fear but not let it dictate our actions or inaction. Pushing our edge requires us to be comfortable within the discomfort and release our need for external validation, anchoring us to our own internal compass of truth.

Six: Darshana — Inspired Vision

Having a vision of what the higher outcome looks and feels like is essential to our path of spiritual growth. When we want to create new patterns, we can create an inner image of our ideal life when we are free of the limiting patterns and beliefs of the ego and subconscious patterns.

Seven: Abhyasa — Persistent Practice

Spiritual growth is not linear. It winds, curves, backslides, and stagnates at times. There are no "failures" or wrong ways on the spiritual path. There are only opportunities to reflect, gain insight, and practice again.

Moving Beyond Limitation

To create lasting change, one needs to cultivate *discipline*, an attitude and actions that are of *service* to others, and consistent *practice* towards one's higher goals. *Discipline* is the fire that drives and is needed to build momentum in a new direction. *Service* to others helps us step out of the limitations of the false ego and into universal connection. Through spiritual *practice*, the unconscious becomes conscious, and we can choose to step out of the patterns that cause suffering in our lives and move into higher states of freedom. It is said that over ninety percent of our cognitive processes are subconscious, operating mostly in the background undetected. Deeply ingrained unconscious beliefs are like ghosts that haunt our consciousness, driving us towards frustration and limiting patterns. Spiritual growth is dependent on awareness and action taken in a positive direction to mature our consciousness and heal the echoes of past trauma that call out from our subconscious and unconscious minds.

Growth takes time and comes in stages. We can look at the progression of the evolution of personal transformation in four stages:

1. **Unconsciously Incompetent:** Before we become aware of limiting beliefs and self-destructive patterns, we are unaware that we lack the skills needed to move out of cycles of suffering.

2. **Consciously Incompetent:** When the pattern is revealed through the light of our awareness, we become aware of the pattern and our

lack of the skills and knowledge required to move into a higher state of living. At this stage, we can seek information and guidance to lead us onto a higher path and a higher perspective. We likely cycle back through the old patterns as we refine our intentions and actions and gather more data to support our new path. Compassion, forgiveness, and grace help us understand that we are not our past behaviors, and we are on a path of learning and discovery.

3. **Consciously Competent:** Once we start to implement our newfound insights, we move out of a pattern of limitation and into a higher state. There is still an awareness of the impulses and momentum of our old habits, but the persistent practice has laid a new path for us to journey on and we become increasingly more confident on our new trajectory.

4. **Unconsciously Competent:** After consistent practice, we fully integrate the new way of being and become completely rooted in our new path. Since we have transformed our subconscious beliefs through spiritual practice, the old ways fade completely into the past and we enjoy our new way of being.

Now you should have a foundational understanding of spirituality, spiritual awakening, and the path out of suffering and bondage. Now we will explore how to apply the practices of spiritual alchemy to catalyze multidimensional awakening and true liberation. Set your intentions and diligently dedicate yourself to your path. Slow yourself down and deepen your awareness. Face the challenges of life with bravery while keeping your inner focus on your inspired vision of Heaven on Earth. There is much love and support for you. Practice! Practice! Practice! All is coming!

FIVE

Meditation

The main tool for spiritual alchemy is the practice of concentration and meditation. Meditation is the experience of single-pointed focus which occurs through practices of mindfulness and concentration. There are countless benefits of practicing meditation including stress relief, liberation from fear of death, development of magnetism in your personality, reduction of heart rate and blood pressure, reduction of inflammation, lowering of cortisol in the body, and elevating spiritual connection. Simply put, meditation helps us create the conditions for the mind to be as useful as possible. When the mind is calm, it translates into the other layers of our being.

In modern society, it is common knowledge that meditation is an excellent tool for personal transformation. The challenge for individuals is twofold. One issue is developing confidence and skill. The other is dedication and commitment to do the practice. My suggestion for those new to meditation is to find a teacher to walk you through the basics of meditation so that you do not get discouraged in the early stages. Then commit to doing the practices for at least 10-20 minutes a day. New Earth Ascending has instructional videos to get you started!

Many different types of meditation exist. Some are passive practices like seated or supine (laying on the back) meditation practices. Some are active movement practices that develop mindful awareness like hatha yoga and qi gong. Try a variety of practices until you find one that feels right and then repeatedly perform that method to unlock its benefits. I highly recommend finding an experienced guide to instruct you with new meditation techniques so that you can quickly develop confidence and skill in the art of meditation. If you find that you have a hard time quieting the mind, combine active practices to regulate and focus the bodymind and then move into stillness practices to go deeper within.

Meditation practices most often involve conscious breathing to unite the physical body and subtle bodies in your awareness. Tuning in to the breath at the beginning of meditation practice is like saddling up on a horse for a journey. Focusing on the breath trains the mind for the journey inward and helps to regulate the autonomic nervous system so that you are relaxed and calm but focused and alert for the journey.

As we progress in meditation practice and throughout our day, we move through five stages of the mind:

1. *Mudham*: dull, forgetful, delusion, and lethargic.
2. *Kshiptam*: raving, wandering, restless, distracted, disturbed state of mind.
3. *Vikshiptam*: oscillating, occasionally steady, easily distracted, thought in process of purification.
4. *Ekaagram*: one-pointed, tranquil, focused, concentrated.
5. *Niruddham*: restrained, cessation of the waves of the mind, controlled, regulated, highly mastered.

Many people give up on meditation because they erroneously believe that they should be able to immediately quiet the mind. When beginning to work with meditative practices, it is expected that a person will naturally be in stages one and two as one develops the awareness and skill needed to move into quieter, more focused states of the mind. Awareness is the first step to creating positive change. The process of developing meditative skill is accelerated when guided by an experienced teacher or when meditating with others. Drop all expectations of what meditation is supposed to look like or feel like and keep practicing stillness and awareness. All is coming!

Meditation Guidelines

Posture

Some practices ask that you are seated with your spine erect. This is not always easy and comfortable for people. I suggest using pillows and blankets to prop yourself into a comfortable position, sitting in a chair, sitting with your back against a wall, or laying down flat if seated positioning is not easy for you. What is important is that the spine is long and that you are comfortable. Seated meditation practice allows the spine to act as an antennae system with the Earth and has many benefits such as strengthening or elongating certain muscle groups, and you are less likely to fall asleep in a seated meditation posture.

Breathe through the Nose

Most breathing practices focus on nasal breathing. Breathing through the nose filters and adjusts the temperature of the air to prepare it to pass through the body. Breathing through the mouth releases life force energy through the moisture that is exhaled in the breath. If you are congested or inhibited in any way, it is perfectly fine to breathe through the mouth.

Diaphragmatic Breathing

The diaphragm is our bridge between the higher spiritual chakras and our lower earthly chakras. When we breathe primarily from our chest, we are ungrounded and floating off the ground. When we focus on initiating breath with the diaphragm and allow the lower abdomen to expand and contract with each breath, this creates a sense of being grounded and connected to the Earth. It also massages our internal organs. To get the most from our breath, we should use "yogic breathing" or three-part breathing to use the full range of movement of breath in the lungs. This is explained more in the *pranamaya kosha* section.

Focus the Mind

Notice all four stages of the breath, including inhalation, retention, exhalation, and suspension. Equalize and extend each stage to create an effortless rhythm. If the mind wanders, bring it back to feeling the sensations of breathing. You can also use affirmations and counting to keep the mind focused on the experience of breathing.

Watching the Breath

The foundation of meditation practice is breath awareness. It is like the horse that you saddle onto for the journey of meditation. As you breathe in and out, deepen your awareness on the experience of breathing. This alone can create powerful energy and clarity. You can use numbers to train the mind into the present moment. For example, breathing in for a count of four, holding for four, exhaling for four, and pausing for four. This trains the mind to be solely focused on the act of breathing. Using a mental mantra or affirmation helps to train the thought patterns to focus on the intention of the meditation. For example, as you breathe in, focus fully on all the sensations of breathing in and mentally say to yourself, "I am aware that I am breathing in." As you exhale, focus fully on all the qualities of breathing out and say to yourself, "I am aware that I am breathing out." This can be simplified to "breathing in" and "breathing out." This practice is my first recommendation for new meditators.

Be Gentle on Yourself

If breathwork or meditative practices add stress to the body or mind, stop immediately, and return to normal breathing. Breathing patterns can be difficult to break. No one is expecting you to master this right away. When you are calm, you can try again.

Emotional Release

It is not uncommon for people to experience a myriad of thoughts, sensations, and emotions as they begin to practice conscious breathing and meditation. Sometimes, powerful emotions can surface that are remnants of unprocessed trauma and past experiences. If this happens, continue to breathe deep and calm breaths and allow the emotional energy to be felt and released.

Energy Movement and Sensations

When we breathe consciously and deeply, we oxygenate the blood and tissues much more than they are used to. This can create tingling sensations, involuntary muscle contractions, heat, and other sensations. Stay calm and continue breathing slowly and deeply to continue moving the energy. If it startles you too much, you can slow down or take a rest.

Basic Meditation Procedure

1. Find a comfortable seated position.
2. Adjust your posture to ensure that you can sit easily for a while with a long, vertical spine. Use props like a wall, meditation pillow, blankets, or a chair to support the body's positioning.
3. Aim for body stillness (*kaya sthairyam*) and progressive relaxation. (Scan the body to soften tension and align the bone structure.)
4. Practice breath awareness (*anapanasati*).
5. Observe the inner planes from a place of witnessing and non-attachment.

6. Add additional practices like *mantra*, breathwork, and visualization to enhance the practice.
7. Experience thoughtless state (move in and out of 6 and 7).
8. Return to waking state of consciousness.

Various Methods of Meditation

Mindfulness Meditation

One type of meditation is mindfulness/witnessing practices. All meditation methods have this quality of paying attention to what arises in one's experience with increasing mental awareness of subtlety and nuance. Mindfulness can be cultivated while breathing, walking, dancing, talking, yoga asana, tai chi, or any other normal day-to-day activities like riding a bike or washing dishes. Every moment holds an opportunity to cultivate mindfulness.

Sublime State Meditation

There is a lot of benefit in simply meditating on the sublime states or virtues such as Peace, Equanimity, Kindness, Compassion, and Joy. Simply evoke the state and supporting imagery in your mind and breathe into it as you allow yourself to bask in the Love and Light of the Sublime.

Antar Mouna: Inner Silence

This meditative practice was made famous by Swami Satyananda, and I discovered additional steps in an article written by yoga teacher trainer Christian Möllenhoff. "*Antar*" means inner and "*mouna*" means stillness. This practice helps you understand the complex functions of the mind so that you can develop a tranquil state of inner silence. The stages of the practice are as follows:

1. Setting up body sturdiness (posture and breath awareness).
2. Externalizing awareness of the senses.
3. Awareness of spontaneous thought processes.
4. Creating thought sequences and willfully stopping them.
5. Awareness and discarding spontaneous thoughts.
6. Awareness of Inner Space (chidakasha) and Emptiness.
7. Alternating between Step 2 and Step 6.
8. Resting in Universal Beingness, Atman.

Mantra Meditation

Another type of meditation is mantra meditation. A person recites, out loud or internally, repetitive thoughts or spoken words that bring the practitioner into loving awareness, unity, and personal empowerment. Many traditions use mantras to create alchemical changes in consciousness, especially in the Tibetan, Vedic, and Jewish traditions. The use of the holy names of the Divine and holy mantras connects the practitioner with the momentum of all the other practitioners who have used these same vibrations throughout all of time and space, including the higher dimensions. These mantras focus the practitioner on higher thoughtforms outside of the mind's conditioning and begin a process of transmutation that happens on all levels of one's being including the DNA. Mantra meditations are also preventative medicine for the consciousness as they protect the mind from absorbing lower thoughtforms.

Mantras or devotional songs in your native language that come from the heart are often the most powerful. If you have any hesitation about reciting mantras in another language, stick with your own language. Here are some mantras from non-English traditions that I have learned that have been helpful in my own healing and transformation. I recommend learning a variety of mantras and devotional songs to infuse many varieties of higher consciousness thoughtforms into your system.

Om/Aum (Sanskrit)

Translates as the primordial sound of Creation, the sound that began all vibrations in Creation. Reciting OM opens the body-mind-Source connection and works at bringing all systems into the original harmonic resonance. Chanting OM alchemically leads us through the four states of consciousness of waking, dreaming, deep sleep, and supreme equilibrium within the sounds of A-U-M and the silence that follows.

Gate Gate Para Gate Parasam Gate Bodhi Svaha (Sanskrit)

"Going, going, going on beyond, always going on beyond, always becoming enlightened"

This mantra connects us to the Higher Evolution of consciousness, moving us from what is currently known and experienced in limitation towards our own Buddhahood and liberated mastery. An extra layer of intention is that recitation of this mantra not only supports your ascension but also extends to assist the ascension of all of life.

Kadoish Kadoish Kadoish Adonai Tsabayoth (Hebrew)

"Holy! Holy! Holy! Lord God of Hosts"

This mantra connects us to the many higher consciousness light beings that serve the Living Light, activating multidimensional transformation for the practitioner.

Lokah Samastah Sukhino Bhavantu (Sanskrit)

"May all beings be free of suffering. May all my words, thoughts, and actions contribute towards that liberation." or *"May all beings be filled with joy, love, and light!"*

Mindful Breathing with Mental Mantra (Ajapa Japa)

Another way to practice is to shift from verbal mantra recitation to mental recitation. Start with a few rounds of your favorite mantra articulating each sound and feeling the meaning and wisdom of the mantra. Then silently repeat the mantra to yourself in your mind while also feeling the meaning and wisdom shining throughout your inner being. In this way, the mantra continues to play in the subconscious throughout the day to elevate the brain patterning.

Trataka Meditation

Another type of meditation is Trataka meditation, which includes focusing one's mind on a single object to induce a trance and inner focus. This is commonly done with a candle, sun gazing, and *yantras* (sacred geometric designs with psychic healing effects). As the practitioner concentrates on the object, they simultaneously remain unattached to any intruding thoughts to develop a state of clarity. Trataka can also be done by imagining that the sacred images or symbols are superimposed on the screen of the mind or in the heart field to bring the qualities of the object of meditation into the inner realm.

When working with a candle, be sure the flame is at eye level, motionless, and that the room is as dark as possible. Stare into the candle while holding meditative awareness. Resist the urge to blink for as long as possible while holding single-pointed focus on the flame. Allow the tears to emerge. When you can no longer hold the gaze, close the eyes and allow the tears to wash through the eyes while holding an inner image of the candle flame. When the image fades, you can begin another round of Trataka. Additionally, you may add mental mantra recitation.

Focusing on an object for even less than a minute cultivates a relaxed mind and a relaxed body. This is commonly experienced in "road hypnosis" when someone loses a chunk of time while driving because of their mind's focus on the road. This also happens when someone is listening to another person speak. We have about twenty to thirty seconds to make a point when we are communicating with others before they start to slip into a hypnotic trance.

I suggest practicing mindfulness if you are watching a TV screen or scrolling through smart devices as these technologies quickly move us into a hypnotic trance with a high level of suggestibility where other thoughts and attitudes can be implanted into our subconscious. When we use these technologies with mindfulness, we know when content is not good for our mind, and we can avoid being programmed subconsciously by changing the content or turning off the device.

Guided Visualization Meditation

Another type of meditation is guided visualization or imaginative meditation using the inner technology of the *chidakasha*, the screen of the mind. In guided visualization, the practitioner visualizes imagery through their imagination to evoke certain emotional experiences such as imagining peaceful scenery like flowing water or sunny fields of flowers to evoke a sense of peace and tranquility. Practitioners can imagine light formations to raise their vibration, like being within a bubble of white light. This practice can be expanded into advanced psychic practices like remote viewing and astral projection as the practitioner learns to project their nonlocal consciousness to other places and times. We do this every night when we sleep as our astral body travels to learn and heal in other realms.

Yoga Nidra

Yoga Nidra is a practice of "yogic sleep" where the practitioner is led through waking consciousness into a deep relaxation that mimics the experience of deep sleep and then intentionally guided back into waking consciousness. This is a great practice to do if you have trouble sleeping or need to take a quick yogic nap to rejuvenate yourself during the day. It is best to have this pre-recorded or have someone lead you through the stages of the process.

Repeated Practice Leads to Mastery

Find a practice or two that you feel resonant with and practice it every day to get used to it. The longer and more consistently you practice, the more benefit and mastery you will experience. After you understand the basics of these practices, you will likely find yourself using them throughout your day. It is perfectly normal to be challenged at first or to have practice sessions that are more challenging with the "monkey mind" jumping from thought to thought. Compassionately accept where you are in your process and keep practicing!

SIX

Koshas: Layers of Being

The human body is a multilayered system of subtle energy fields of various vibrational frequencies that are in a constant state of transformation. What people typically call their "body" is actually several different bodies overlapping one another. *Kosha* is a Sanskrit word for "sheaths" as it describes the different bodies fitting into one another like a sword into its scabbard. Each one fits inside the other like Russian nesting dolls or a hand fitting into a glove. Each layer is inserted into, pervades, and extends beyond the previous. Each exists in its own bandwidth, its own density, from the most physical to the ultradimensional part of us that exists beyond this illusory world. We are truly multidimensional holographic beings of Light!

The term 'holarchy' is a word created by fusing together 'whole' and 'hierarchy' to describe individual components which have their own wholeness but contribute to a greater wholeness and unification. The human body is a mirror reflection of the greater cosmological order. Just as Source is the greater sphere which all other spheres of creation exist within, the Source within us lays the foundation for the other layers of our being to emerge.

While each layer is whole and has its own functions and properties, each layer contributes to the greater wholeness of our being. We separate each layer to understand its components, functions, and purpose, yet we should keep in mind that each layer contributes to the entire hologram of our being and all layers interpenetrate, occupy the same space, and work in symbiotic relationship so that our soul can have the experience of physicality and evolution.

Different traditions have different classifications and numbers of layers of the *koshas*. Most traditions have between four to seven distinctly different layers of the aura of our consciousness vehicle. They mostly describe them as the same but separate some layers into sublayers.

After looking at several philosophies, I have come to find great value in the Advaita Vedanta model of consciousness, as well as the contemporary models presented in Theosophy, the work of Meher Baba, and other lineages. The following theoretical model is a fusion combining the wisdom from my research.

Three-Body System

The human form can be separated into three different major bodies which can be separated into different planes of consciousness. The base for these layers is the Source Self which projects other layers to experience Creation. Note that I categorize these slightly differently than Vedanta. The three major layers are:

1. *Physical Body:* Physical, Material layer
2. *Subtle Body:* Etheric layer, conscious mind, subconscious
3. *Causal Body:* superconscious mind, buddhi, auric film

Some occult traditions break this into the categories of body, soul, and Spirit. The soul is the lightbody which is the combination of the subtle bodies and causal body from my model. This soul is what moves from life to life. The Spirit is the Atman/Self/Source, which is Absolute, omnipresent, omnipotent, and ever free. This is your True Nature.

The Causal Consciousness Body, the most subtle body is the first layer that manifests and is the seed layer from which the other layers emerge. It holds the karmic imprints and mental patterns from past lives which lie dormant until triggered by life experiences. The causal body gives birth to the subtle body, which create the template matrix for the physical body, which is the medium through which the soul experiences the Material Realm. In the model I use, the causal consciousness body includes the superconscious mind functions, the higher mind that is cultivated in spiritual awakening.

The Subtle Consciousness Body gives us the capacity to feel and sense our experience. This grouping of layers is made of the etheric structuring of the physical body as well as the functions of the conscious and subconscious mind. The subtle body gives us access to the subtle realms and bridges us with the higher consciousness planes. It is the layer in which universal *prana* enters our body and is converted for life processes. In some traditions, the life force layer (*pranamaya kosha*) is combined with the physical layer to create one "body of action." In other traditions, the pranic layer is considered part of the Subtle Body. I find understanding in both. For the sake of the ease of this transmission, I will link the vital layer with the Subtle Body.

According to Vedanta, the subtle body is said to have nineteen or seventeen main components, depending on the lineage of the teaching. In this system the higher and lower mind functions belong to the subtle body. The components include:

- five organs of knowledge (eyes, ears, nose, tongue, skin)
- five organs of action (mouth, hands, legs, genitals, anus),
- five pranas (*prana, apana, vyana, udana, samana)*. I will also note the chakras and nadis here.
- four internal organs (mind/*manas*, memory/*chitta*, *intellect/*buddhi*, *ego/*ahamkara*).

The Physical Body exists in the physical plane. It is the densest layer and is made of all the physical organs, tissues, and their processes. It is the physical vehicle for soul, our subtle bodies, to experience physical life through. The transcendental Self, the Atman, pervades each layer, conducting the orchestration of all systems at once. Our True Nature, our True Self, is that One Light of Consciousness, the Awareness and Witness of all objects of experience including the bodymind and the world.

Within the three major bodies are the subplanes of each plane of existence with different functions that contribute to the whole. If there is curiosity, I recommend researching the lineages that I have sourced this wisdom from.

- **Physical Consciousness Body**
  - o *Annamaya Kosha*: Physical Layer: Material Sheath
- **Subtle Consciousness Body**
  - o *Pranamaya Kosha*: Vital Layer: Pranic Sheath
  - o *Kamamaya Kosha*: Conscious Mind: Desire Sheath
  - o *Manomaya Kosha*: Subconscious Mind: Mental Sheath
- **Causal Consciousness Body**
  - o *Atimanasa Kosha*: Supramental Mind: Intuitive Sheath
  - o *Vijnanamaya Kosha*: Subliminal Mind: Intellectual Sheath
  - o *Anandamaya Kosha*: Subtle Causal Mind: Bliss Sheath
  - o *Atman*: Pure Consciousness, Source within, Spirit

It is a common belief that we are a physical body that can have spiritual experiences, but the truth is we are a spiritual being that experiences ourselves in form. We originate beyond form and develop a causal body, subtle body, and physical body. In this way, we can think of these sheaths as layers of ignorance that distract us from perceiving the Atman/Source/Self, but they do not cover the Self because our True Nature is all-pervasive, vast, limitless, and unblockable. We just need to quiet the noise of the mind and senses to notice what is always there in the background of our awareness. We are Source right here, right now, and forever.

These coverings inhibit us from experiencing the knowledge of the Source Self. Our Source Self "sits" in the background witnessing the different bandwidths of density overlaying our Divine Nature. We are not the body that walks about this world of solid form. We are not the "breathing body" of vital energy and its vital processes. We are not the thinking consciousness, the egoic identity, or our memories and desires. We are not the intellectual processes of our higher mind. We are not even the blankness of the bliss consciousness. We are the Seer of all experiences. We are the pure Consciousness that observes them all. We are the Witness of these illusory phenomena, pure unbridled beingness. Through the process of Ascension, we are not rejecting the body or mind but elevating it to the highest capacity and functioning so that the full Light of our Being can shine through each kosha.

These sheaths are symbiotic, working together to create the vessel that you experience life through. These systems are always working toward harmony and vitality to create a resonant, unified field of pure light. This state of balance is called homeostasis, made through the harmonic organization and coherence of each sheath. As you come into deeper awareness of each layer and reconcile its distortions, the healing benefits spread to the other bodies so that the whole system benefits from improvements. This next section will take you through each of the koshas and provide thorough instructions on how to purify and strengthen each of these bodies in preparation for Ascension.

Moving from the Unreal to the Real

The koshas are the robes that Jesus spoke about when he taught of cleaning the robes to prepare for the next garment of Light. What we eat, what we give our life force to, and the thoughts we think affect our ability to tune into the brilliance of our Divine Nature.

Why do we not know our True Nature? We are confused and ignorant of our true beingness because of our misperceptions, misidentifications, and the roles connected to each of the koshas. Our awareness is focused on and distracted by our own *samsara*, our own suffering mind-body complex. We have become enamored and intoxicated by the dream spell of *maya*.

To understand our True Nature, to know what we ARE, we can negate or remove the layers of what we are NOT. As we peel back the layers of our *koshas* like we peel the layers of an onion, we arrive at the true knowledge of who we are as pure Consciousness.

In Advaita Vedanta there is an understanding that the True Nature is the Atman, the transcendental Self, which is Brahman (Source) having an experience in form as the individual self. The Atman is the Seer of Creation, so it can never be seen as an object or reduced to a form. It is the Atman, the Source within us, which gives us sentience, the awareness to witness the ever-shifting forms and names within one's experience. The pure Consciousness is stable, changeless, and ever-present. If your True Self is the subjective consciousness, sentient (aware), and changeless, we can test each of the *koshas* to see that they do not match these criteria. The physical body cannot be aware of the Source. The Etheric Body is constantly changing. The higher and lower mind faculties disappear in deep sleep and our experiences of bliss and unity come and go. Yet it is our self-luminous Self that shines the Light of awareness on all of these ever-shifting experiences.

The words we speak are like spells that can either move us into higher states of expansion or they can anchor us into the illusion even more. Every time we say the words "I am..." the words that follow have an immediate effect and can show us which layer of our personality we are identifying with. When we say, "I am ugly," we are identifying with the physical body. When we say, "I am exhausted," we are identifying with our vital energy system. When we say, "I am mad," we are identifying with the emotional body. "I am confused," we are identifying with the mental body. Yet, all the while, the soul still shines as Pure Consciousness. A more accurate statement would be "I am pure consciousness experiencing this body, vitality, and the manifestations of thought and insight." You are ever the witness and never the witnessed. You are pure consciousness itself!

When we get our awareness overly involved in the different layers of our personality, their roles, and the manifestations in those layers, we overlook our Divine Self. It is a paradox in that the spiritual journey is one of seeking and looking for the "Truth of Who I Am," yet Source is always there. Our True Self is always present, yet most of humanity consciously or unconsciously decides to "look the other way" and gets caught up in associating with the distractions of the different layers of density that make up the koshas. Yet, at some point we "hear the call" of our divine nature saying "Come, find me." and the spiritual journey begins. We begin to remember the mission of ascension that we planned for ourselves before we entered this physical world. We begin to turn away from the "ways of the world" and begin to seek fulfillment from living a spiritualized life focused on awakening to the True Nature of reality.

How do we free ourselves from our limited egoic identity, spiritual ignorance, and karmic prison? There are infinite ways! Every spiritual wisdom tradition has ways of focusing one's life towards the Higher Consciousness. The yogic sciences encourage us to fine-tune our awareness and action towards altruistic actions that serve the good of all (*karma yoga*). We can balance the polarities of our bodymind complex (*hatha yoga*). We can grow in devotion to and our love of God (*bhakti yoga*). We can meditate on our Divine Nature and the Divine Reality (*raja yoga*). We can infuse our minds with Divine Knowledge (*jnana yoga*). While these names are Sanskrit terms, similar concepts can be found in all wisdom and faith traditions.

From the perspective of linear time, our many incarnations evolved our individual consciousness by progressing from the simplest to most complex consciousness forms to the point of taking human form. In human form, we can begin the process of liberating our consciousness in what is called God-realization, Self-realization, or Ascension. Even though the divine presence of our True Being is always there, yet it requires seeking, searching, and spiritual practice to fully establish ourselves in that pure Consciousness state. For most, it takes many lifetimes to fully realize what we have always been.

It is said at the highest state of realization, we live in the knowing that we were never caught in karma, we were never born and never died. All was just an appearance, a game of Light and shadow we played with our Oneself. We have always been free, we are free, and we will always be free we just have not yet noticed it through direct experience and embodied knowledge.

The next portion of the book takes you deeper into each layer so that you can uncover the treasure that lies within the core of your being and permeates every atom of your physical form. As we journey through these layers of our personality, we find that the Kingdom of Heaven lives within our very being! Take a moment to still the body and quiet the mind and listen to your inner dimension and see what is already there. What you seek is closer than you think.

SEVEN

Annamaya Kosha: Physical Body

When most people think of who they are, they think of the physical body. This is the matter, muscles, skin, bones, connective tissues, organs, blood, cells, DNA, etc. The physical vessel is transient and passes through the stages of birth, growth, degeneration, and physical death. The *annamaya kosha* is related to the Root Chakra, your physical DNA, and your maternal and paternal ancestral lines. This dense energy envelope is made of the food you eat and is the vehicle for our Source Self to experience physicality. At the base level of the physical body, you find the five elemental energies of earth, water, fire, air, and space/ether which organize in countless ways to create things like bone structure, bodily fluids, digestive power, movement of breath, and the space that surrounds and separates the many parts and systems of the body. This body is not who we truly are. From ashes to ashes, dust to dust, five elements to five elements it will go. Yet, we are eternal.

Experiencing the Matrix of Existence

Our movement through the activities of our life is powered through a multidimensional exchange of energy information. Energy information passes through the physical sense organs of our eyes, skin, ears, tongue, nose and brain which give us the perceptual power to experience the subtle elements of form, touch, sound, taste, and smell. As this energy information is processed from the physical body into the subtle body via the etheric structuring of the *pranamaya kosha*. It is then directed into the mind where it is experienced, processed, and stored. Almost immediately impulses of desire and willpower ripple out through the mind into the vital energy structures and our physical brain and body to direct physical processes and the organs of action which include the mouth, hands, feet, excretory organs, and reproductive organs.

The physical vessel is constantly receiving energy information and transforming it into useful data for the body systems. The systems of the physical body include the skeletal, muscular, nervous, endocrine, respiratory, reproductive, immune, urinary, digestive, circulatory, cardiovascular, lymphatic, and integumentary systems. This complex network of systems is always working towards harmony and balance called homeostasis.

Illness and Disease

Physical illness is a manifestation of dense, toxic energy eliminated through the symptoms of the illness. The root of all illness, disorder, and disease can be found in the subtle bodies as manifestation is always energetic before it becomes physical. We think a certain way, which energizes our body into speech and action which move us into situations of balance or imbalance, health or disease. Even hereditary illness is an echo of thoughts and karmic actions passed down through our genetic lineages and humanity's collective unconscious. Latent mental patterning stored in the Causal Body can also be reactivated by our environment causing us to recreate injuries and illness from past lives.

Our health is affected by the things we see, the quality of the air we breathe, the things we eat, the sounds we hear, and the things we put on our skin. We are inundated with toxins from our environment and distorted programming from the mainstream industries. Many people live in areas of pollution and eat poisonous food. Finding natural solutions and detoxifying our bodies is essential for Ascension to ensure a clean and clear Ascension vessel, the physical body.

Understanding Stress

One of the major causes of physical body imbalance is stress. Stress is a feeling of mental, emotional, or physical tension that occurs as we face the challenges of living. In some cases, stress can be healthy and drive us to accomplish our goals. Stress can also be detrimental to our health, such as enduring traumatic conditions or unhealthy mental pressure from the conditioning of the mind.

Stress and anxiety wreak havoc on the systems of our body and consciousness. Erratic emotions, body tension, fearful thinking, and unhealthy behavioral patterns are symptoms of us being out of balance.

Mindfulness and wellness practices move our bodymind systems out of stagnation and decay into regenerative states of cohesion, balance, and flow.

Stress, real or imagined, has an immediate effect on all body systems, including the nervous system, digestive system, reproductive system, respiratory system, mental cognition, and so on. One of the keys to understanding stress and stress management is through the autonomic nervous system. Following is a summary of the components and functions of our autonomic nervous system and how we create stress or harmony through our physiology.

Autonomic Nervous System

The autonomic nervous system (ANS) regulates bodily functions such as breathing rate, heart rate, digestion, urination, and pupillary response. This system helps us adjust to daily living demands from a place of stress and anxiety or a place of flow and balance. The ANS acts mostly unconsciously and has two subsystems that create the "fight, flight, or freeze" responses of the body (sympathetic nervous system) or the "rest and digest" response (parasympathetic nervous system).

Sympathetic Nervous System

The sympathetic nervous system (SNS) is activated when the body and mind are under stress. This could be from actual stressors in our environment like toxins, loud noises, or stressful situations. This can also happen when the mind drifts into memories of past stress or projects stressful outcomes in the future.

When our sympathetic nervous system is activated, our digestive system stops working, and the blood is redirected to the arms and legs so that we can fight our stress or run from it. In this stage of ANS response, our heart rate elevates and becomes erratic. When our body and mind are in various stress states, we switch from deeper diaphragmatic breathing to shallow upper chest breathing as the sympathetic nervous system activates.

With the diaphragm frozen in movement, the upper chest and neck muscles pull on the rib cage to make space for the lungs to expand. This results in shorter, shallow breathing that leaves our neck and chest muscles tight and agitated. Our autonomic nervous system often stays in fight or flight response way after the initial stressful experience partly because the respiratory system stays locked in defense mode while our subconscious stores the unprocessed energy information. This creates trapped emotions that continue to oscillate in one's mental field creating tremors of reactivation within the bodymind complex.

Modern Western society is a product of the SNS where everyone is fighting to survive or climb an invisible social ladder. We are inundated with blatant and subliminal messages that we are not enough, and our future is bleak. This constant stress manifests as chronic illness, emotional disorders, and beyond. One of the most radical things you can do to unplug from this machine's momentum is to develop mindful breathing and presence.

Parasympathetic Nervous System

When our parasympathetic nervous system (PNS) is activated, our heart rate slows down, our breathing deepens, our digestive system runs smoothly, and our overall mood and mind are balanced. When our body and mind are calm and relaxed, we naturally use our diaphragm for breathing, allowing our lower abdomen to expand and contract. This movement and type of breathing are easily seen by observing an infant or sleeping dog.

Diaphragmatic breathing is natural and effortless for the body. The diaphragm, like the heart, can continue contracting and releasing without tiring or needing rest. When we practice diaphragmatic breathing, our respiratory organs and digestive organs are massaged, cleansed, and toned by the rhythmic movement caused by the expansion of the diaphragm and lungs.

Vagus Nerve

The vagus nerve system of neural pathways originates in the brain stem and weaves a serpentine pathway through the body, touching upon various vital organs and neural networks before it fractals out into the intestines. This family of neural pathways interacts with the *hara line/sushumna and* chakras to send information to the brain to modulate emotions, translate intuitive "gut" instincts, create bodily sensations, inform relationship responses, and activate processes for environmental adaptation.

The Dance of the Autonomic Nervous System

The vagus nerve plays a significant part in transferring from the SNS (sympathetic nervous system) to the PNS (parasympathetic nervous system). "Vagal tone" is our ability to respond to stressors in our life. When the vagal tone is low and unhealthy, we are quickly agitated and stressed out by life. When the vagal tone is high and healthy, we can quickly and easily manage life stressors and return to the states of homeostasis and flow.

Activities for increasing vagal tone: dancing, yoga, meditation, massage, singing, chanting, prayer, cold exposure (cold shower), positive social connections, and other relaxing and inspiring activities.

We are constantly shifting in and out of PNS and SNS responses. Both the SNS and PNS are activated within a single breath cycle. As we inhale, the SNS activates, causing our heart rate to increase. We feel alert, active, and inspired during the inhalation phase. As we exhale, the PNS activates, causing our heart rate to lower and the vagal response to increase. As we exhale, we soften, relax, and settle into ourselves. There is nothing wrong or bad about the SNS, we just should not live there out of habit, or we will likely fry our systems.

Conscious breathing directs our mental awareness to our experience of breathing, where we can become conscious influencers of our autonomic nervous system. When we link our awareness with our breath, we almost automatically switch to calmer, deeper breathing, and a more balanced state of being. As our parasympathetic nervous system activates through conscious, diaphragmatic breathing, all our body systems begin to balance and restore.

When someone takes a "sigh of relief," this is the bodymind complex releasing the physical, vital, and mental responses to the stressful experience. Deep sighs of relief are signs that the ANS is switching from SNS to a PNS response. Walking in nature, meditation, physical exercise, and spending quiet time alone all help the PNS activate and restore our body systems to homeostasis, coherence, and flow.

One of the best ways to increase vagal tone and increase our vital energy is through conscious embodiment practices like meditation and yoga. Conscious breathing practices are simple tools we can use to regulate subtle energy in our body systems and establish states of rejuvenation and calm presence. These are spoken of more in the *pranamaya kosha* section, and the mental component of stress is discussed more deeply in the section on the *manomaya kosha.*

Physical Body Focuses for Ascension

The physical layer of our personality will be transforming with us as we transmigrate from this dimensional reality to the next. The biological and subtle energy processes of ascension need nourishment to ensure an easy transition. Below are a few keys regarding the physical layer maintenance through the ascension process.

Physical Body Training

Physical training and self-care should incorporate a balance of active and passive activities to regulate the autonomic nervous system, develop overall strength and flexibility, and reduce stress and neuromuscular tension.

For those who tend to have higher levels of stress and body tension, passive practices such as restorative yoga, self-massage, sound healing, journaling, and long baths can be added to activate the parasympathetic nervous response to calm the bodymind. Long, gentle stretching helps to loosen the connective tissues of the body to create harmonic flow in the physical and subtle body systems.

For those who need to develop strength and willpower, active practices such as working out at the gym, martial arts, hatha yoga, and brisk walking help to energize and strengthen the body. Active practices help to develop muscle tone, increase coordination and create movement in the organs and tissues of the body for healthy elimination and detoxification.

Overall, each individual's practices and life activities should be a balance between movement and stillness, active and passive, fast and slow to bring the bodymind systems into harmony and cohesion.

Self-Massage Practice

There are a variety of ways to do self-massage. Here is a short description of a self-massage practice to improve circulation, balance overall skin health, reduce stress, and so much more. Go slow. Enjoy the sensuality and use it as a practice of devotion towards yourself, your body, and beyond.

1. Use warmed organic oils like coconut oil, sesame, or something similar. You may wish to use organic essential oils as well.
2. Start at the scalp and work your way down to the collarbone. Use the fingertips to make tiny circles. Pay special attention to Crown, Brow, Zeal, and Throat Chakras.
3. Progress from fingertips to shoulder with long strokes on the limbs and short, circular strokes at the joints. Repeat on the other arm.
4. Employ the same concept from feet to hips.
5. Massage the abdomen with clockwise strokes.
6. Massage across the low back/sacral.
7. Rub center of the chest outward.
8. Pause for 5-10 minutes. Bonus if you use Reiki on yourself or meditate during that time.
9. Rinse with a cold/cool shower.

Diet and Water Intake

Every human body is different in what it needs to sustain itself through this process. Whatever you ingest, try your best to have organic foods that are grown locally and ethically. It has been suggested that we eliminate dairy because it creates a distortion in the energy layers that makes energy upgrades difficult. Plant-based diets are most recommended but if you must eat meat, make sure the animal was raised humanely and organically. Be sure to give thanks to the life expression of that being for its sacrifice.

Foods should be living and fresh, not processed or from cans. Supplements are recommended to ensure that you are getting all the nutrients that you need. Superfoods that have high nutritional value help keep everything vibrant and healthy.

Water is super important for the alchemical transformation of Ascension. Spring water or from other pure natural water sources is the best, and it is recommended to add hydration salts and trace minerals if using purified water. Municipal water sources should be avoided as the water is most likely highly contaminated with chemicals that negatively affect the body and mind.

It is recommended to perform intermittent fasting and periodic detoxification protocols to rid the body of toxic waste. These are excellent to start around the full moon as the waning movement helps with the release of physical, energetic, and mental patterns that are not of the highest benefit to your well-being.

Take time to pray over your food. Hold your hands above the food and envision Light shining from your hands and/or your brow chakra to enhance and purify the food. Send gratitude to all the forces and beings that played a part in bringing you your meal. Eat mindfully, slowly, and allow yourself to have a multidimensional experience as you eat.

Proper Rest and Sleep

Proper rest is important for optimal physical, vital, and mental well-being. Everyone is different with how many hours are needed for rest. Find ways to increase the length of time in the blankness of deep sleep. This includes limiting screen time before bed and reducing the amount of stimulants and caffeine taken into the body. Have a self-reflection and winding down practice to get the body ready for rest. This will help to clear the mind so that you are not too active in dream states and can spend more time in the state of dreamless sleep.

Progressive Relaxation Body Scan

Progressive relaxation practices help develop body consciousness and an overall feeling of deep relaxation. The fascial grid is a network of connective tissue that surrounds all the muscles, organs, tendons, and even the bones. Our bodies have many habitual holding patterns which limit the free flow of subtle energy throughout our system. The fascial grid acts as a passageway for vital energy. Holding patterns in any area of the grid limit the free flow of vital energy and cause disruption and imbalance. As you practice this body scan, imagine the whole fascial network softening to allow the free flow of subtle energy.

Progressive Relaxation Body Scan Procedure

- Lay down or recline in a comfortable position.
- Breathe into the naval center, diaphragmatic breathing, for a few rounds to settle into your body.

- Feel the breath in the throat for a few rounds and set intention to relax the bodymind.
- Breath into the nostrils and allow yourself to settle into even deeper subtle consciousness. Take this profound feeling of relaxation and focus throughout the body scan. Take your time and enjoy the process.
- Relax the scalp and crown of your head.
- Relax the muscles of your face.
- Relax the forehead, eyebrows, and eyes.
- Relax your cheeks, tongue, mouth, jaw, chin, throat, and neck.
- Relax your shoulders, upper arms, elbows, lower arms, wrists, hands, and fingers (rest for five breaths).
- Relax your heart center and sides of chest
- Relax your solar plexus and stomach.
- Relax your lower abdomen, pelvis, pubic bone, pelvic floor, and lower back.
- Relax your upper legs, lower legs, ankles, feet, and toes (waiting here for five breaths).
- Reverse the process back up to the crown without pausing. Relax for several breaths and slowly return to waking consciousness by deepening the breath and moving the fingertips and toes tips.

Bless Your Body

Before incarnation, you chose the perfect genetics to experience this life through. Love this physical body and treat it well as it is the temple of your Divine Light. Celebrate the body and dedicate it towards your higher purpose, using it as an instrument for your liberation. Enjoy your senses; enjoy your path; and dedicate your physical vessel's life expressions towards the liberation of all beings from cycles of suffering!

EIGHT

Pranamaya Kosha: Pranic Body

In the beginning stages of spiritual awakening, we begin to realize that there is something more to physical life than what can be experienced with the physical senses and mainstream reality structure. We begin to sense something mystical to life and begin to turn inward to listen to our inner realm and tune into the interconnectedness of life.

As we awaken, we begin to discover that we exist within a unified field of light and vibration, a continuum of energy that is constantly shifting and changing through an infinite latticework of geometric grid patterns which mesh together to create the holographic matrix of the universe. When I use the word 'energy' throughout this book, subtle energy is what I speak of. Subtle energies are the substratum of all manifestations in Creation and act as the organizing principle, providing the pathways and movements of Consciousness as it evolves within the Unified Field of Creation. Subtle energy is interactive with our own consciousness. As we focus on it, it begins to transform immediately as it links with our consciousness giving us the ability to transfer will and intent across time and space such as in prayer and psychic phenomena.

It should be mentioned that not all energy is "good energy." There are seemingly negative, entropic energies that take away life force, and there are positive, centropic energies that sustain and revitalize life. These energies aren't "good" or "bad" as each frequency serves a purpose or function. The "problem" with energy comes when things are out of sync with Natural Order and are not able to balance and integrate back into wholeness.

In Samkhya, dualistic Vedic philosophy, there is the pure Self, *purusha*, and matter and form, *prakriti*. *Prakriti, maya* consists of three fundamental forces: *sattva, rajas,* and *tamas*. These forces called *gunas,* translated as "strand" or "fiber," are the threads that weave the web of the manifestation of the cosmos. All phenomena that can be experienced, seen and unseen, is a manifestation of the weaving of the matrix with the force of the *gunas in conjunction with the subtle and gross elements of earth, air, fire, water, and ether (space)*.

These forces can be described as follows:

- *sattva*: harmony, purity, light, beauty, balance, consciousness revelation, balance, inspiration
- *rajas*: change, activity, active energy, unsteadiness, movement, agitation, transitions us to sattvic or tamasic
- *tamas*: darkness, conceals consciousness, ignorance, depression, dullness, stagnation, inertia, stability, mindless, intoxicating, inaction

All of these forces can be positive when in balance with the other forces. Ultimately, we should be guiding our experience into sattvic states of balance and inspiration versus the downward spirals that leads to ignorance, decay, and stagnation.

Most ancient cultures have various ways of accessing, manipulating, and understanding the many subtle energy categories and their qualities. There are many names in many cultures for subtle energy. *Ki* (Japanese), *prana* (Sanskrit), *chi* (Chinese), *ruach* (Hebrew), and *life force energy* (English) are just a few.

Prana is the animating life force of the physical body and the active power behind all vital phenomena in the universe. We receive this "breath of life" from the food and water we ingest, our environment, our inhalations of breath, and from our soul and higher consciousness connection. While *prana* is necessary for biological life to exist, too much of it causes nervousness and psychosis and in the most extreme case death. Having too little of it causes exhaustion, and our physical life is over when there is no longer *prana* in the physical body.

Alchemical practices like tantra, yoga, qi gong, and the laying of hands work with subtle energy to restore balance and harmony to a person's physical, vital, and mental bodies to create homeostasis and alignment with one's True Nature. Group prayer and ceremonies create a powerful energy field that amplifies prayers and intentions, and many people experience spontaneous healing and emotional healing through the group prayer field.

Many people who have not had a subtle energy experience of their own find it hard to believe that subtle energy exists, believing in only what they see with their physical eyes. Many reject the idea of a subtle energy reality. Scientific communities are beginning to develop instruments that can measure subtle energy. Many hospitals and clinics in the West are now beginning to allow practitioners of acupuncture and hands-on healing methods like Reiki into the hospital system to support patients' recovery.

Simple Energy Exercise

One of the best tools to sense and interact with subtle energy is with the hands. The awareness is amplified when you apply conscious breathing to the task.

Bring your palms together and begin to rub them vigorously while you consciously breathe in and out of your belly. Close your eyes and feel the sensations. Intend to generate powerful energy and heat. Use your breath and intention to amplify the vibrations, intending for the energy field to grow stronger and brighter. After a few moments, begin to open your hands slowly. Tune into the sensations between your hands. What do you feel? What do you sense? Trust your feelings. Can you feel both the electric and magnetic qualities? Warm or cold sensations? Tingling? This is a form of subtle energy. You can take your hands and lightly move them across your face and body and sense the energy there. When finished, keep the awareness, and open the eyes.

The Human Energy System

Inserted in the physical body and extending slightly beyond is the vital body, also called the etheric body or pranic body. The human body is a multidimensional bio-transducer, meaning it constantly receives, transforms, and emits various levels of subtle energy. The vital energy system translates energy information into the physical systems to create physical body functions like heart rate, hormone release, breathing rate, and beyond. This sheath bridges our physical body with our mental body by translating subtle energy information for physical and mental processes.

In Theosophy, this layer is called the Etheric Body Double because it is similar in shape and size to the physical body. Every cell of the body, every particle of bodily fluids, bodily gas, and organic material is surrounded by an etheric energy envelope that weaves a matrix of pathways to unify all systems. As information streams in through the physical sense experiences, information is passed from the cells into the etheric double of the cells and is translated through subtle information pathways to the etheric brain and mental body. Higher consciousness information and mental patterning experienced in the mental body are transmitted through the etheric pathways and etheric brain into the physical brain and nervous system to direct the body's actions and functions.

Aura: Your Personal Space

All living organisms have an auric field which is called a biofield in science. The human biofield is a toroidal field of electromagnetic light that emanates from the core of your being and creates the matrix framework for your physical body. The aura includes the etheric structuring of the *pranamaya kosha* as well as the oscillation and activities of the mental and causal bodies. Our aura is multilayered and is in constant evolution and transformation based on our mood, thoughts, the food we eat, location, etc. Our auric field is the instrument we use to interact with the subtle energy world around us. It receives energy information from outside of our physical body and radiates energy information into the Unified Field of Creation. Our overall light quotient in our auric field is dependent on the health of all our koshas. Our auric field becomes unstable and distorted when we are in states of aggression, sadness, or other lower emotions. Our auric field is harmoniously organized and coherent when we are in higher vibrational states like joy, creativity, and devotion.

Aura Experience

Close your eyes and begin to focus on your breath and the subtle sensations of your experience. Call the Light to be with you and feel your vibration begin to rise. Imagine that within your heart center, in the core of your being, is a sacred fire, a beautiful bright Light of Source Energy. Use your intention, focus, and breathing to expand this source of energy until it surrounds you. Make your space feel beautiful and loving and filled with light. Deep, full breathing amplifies the radiance and love from this Light. Allow your thoughts to be purified and your mind relaxed by this Light. Feel your intention to merge with the Light and evoke feelings of peace and tranquility. Amplify these positive sensations with your breathing. Notice how far your personal energy field goes. Is it a bubble or does it fade out into the space around you? Feel the energy within you. Notice any stagnant areas, and breathe light and awareness into them, inviting movement and flow.

As you inhale, pull your field back into the core of your being. As you exhale, pulse your light back out. Keep repeating this pattern as if you are flexing your etheric muscles. With each exhale, your aura is brighter, cleaner, and more pronounced. Enjoy this for as long as you desire. When you are complete, feel your aura strong and illuminated. Feel blessed by the experience and open your eyes.

Boundaries

It is important to do frequent aura clearing and restructuring throughout the day, especially if you live a hectic life. Having healthy, energetic boundaries ensures that we do not take on the energy of other people and places. Having a clear aura helps you to have clear thoughts and a joyful mood. Practices like smudging or spraying "aura mists" over the body help to clear and recharge the energy field. It is especially important to intentionally restructure and strengthen your energy field when you go into public so that you remain sovereign and clear of others' energy.

Five Movements of the Breath of Life

We access and regulate the *pranamaya kosha* through the act of breathing, our main source of *prana,* and intentionally through the power of our mind. As this universal life force enters our body it is separated into five "winds" with different movement patterns and functions. These five pranic winds stimulate all bodily processes and govern our health and vitality. Any disruptions or imbalances in the flow of these life force patterns manifest on both the physical and mental planes of our personality. The five major movements of *prana* in the body are as follows:

One: Incoming Energy

Prana vayu, located in the region of the head and chest, moves inward and upward and deals with inspiration, intake, receptivity, and forward momentum and is associated with the heart chakra and brow chakra and the air element. Prana enters through the organs of perception from the food we eat, the air we breathe, the sights we see, the sounds we hear, and through the skin. Imbalances may present as dysfunction in the lungs, heart, brain, and circulatory system.

Two: Outgoing Energy

Apana vayu, located in the pelvic region and lower abdomen, expels downward and outward, deals with elimination movements like perspiration, defecation, and urination. It directs the reproductive processes of ejaculation, menstruation, and childbirth and is associated with the organs below the naval. It is associated with the *muladhara chakra*, the Root Center, and the earth element. Imbalances manifest as dysfunction in organs of elimination and reproduction.

Three: Digestive Energy

Samana vayu, located between the navel and heart, is the balancing energy of the body which deals with multidimensional digestion and assimilation processes and is associated with the *manipura chakra*, the solar plexus, and the element of fire. *Samana vayu* draws energy into the solar plexus center for processing our food, subtle energy, thoughts, and energy from the physical holographic reality. Imbalances can manifest as over or underactive digestive patterns, abdominal discomfort, and gas.

Four: Upward Energy

Udana vayu, located in the throat, has an upward movement and deals with speech, expression, growth, and the upward ascension of prana and kundalini. Associated with the *vishuddha chakra*, *udana vayu* emanates from the throat center in a circular motion around the neck and head, thus assisting with mental clarity and focus. It directs the self-transformation process and the recalibration of willpower to a higher purpose and vision. Imbalances manifest as dysfunction in the throat, neck, and head.

Five: Circulation Energy

Vyana vayu, located in and around the whole body, has an outward from center movement pattern and deals with circulation, expansiveness, and pervasiveness as it directs subtle energy throughout the 72,000 pathways of subtle energy called *nadis* which physicalize as communication networks like the nerves and fascial grid. This movement provides a connection between the senses, nerves, tissues, cells, and the mind creating a feeling of wholeness and containment. This circulatory movement is associated with the *svadhisthana chakra*, the sacral center, and the element of water. Imbalances manifest as feeling unstable, containerless, and clumsy. Overall, the imbalance manifests as systemic dysfunctions of the body

There is an ancient saying that says something like, "If you can extend the length of your breath, you can extend the length of your life." Our quality of breathing, from day to day, determines our quality of living. As we train the breath, we become more radiant and vital. Many spiritual and mystical traditions revere the transformative power of the breath. Life can be thought of as one long breath cycle starting from the first inhalation as a newborn to the last breath of life. Breathing transforms our experience of time. Fast, shallow breathing is parallel to the experience of rush or not enough time. Slow and steady breathing brings us to the present moment where time endlessly unfolds in the eternal NOW.

Hara Line: Bridging Heaven and Earth

You are connected to universal life force and the regenerative consciousness field of Gaia by a pillar of Light that passes through the center of the body, which I call the hara line or pranic tube, or the sushumna nadi when speaking about the physical body. This pranic tube is the axis of the toroidal field of your auric field.

This subtle energy tube tethers us to the subtle planes and the electromagnetic fields of planet Earth. This is our lifeline and our connection to our battery. When we are in the states of love and trust, this pathway is open and clear. When we are in the states of fear and separation consciousness, we are severed from our battery, and we lose life force.

Our hara line, our pranic tube, is the main intake and outtake pathway of our subtle energy body and supplies our chakras with energy from Source and Gaia. When we have a healthy hara line, we feel centered in our being, connected to Source and Gaia, and alive and aligned with our Divine Purpose and the Divine Will of the Universe. We feel energized, alert, and connected to Higher Love.

When our hara line is distorted and blocked, we can feel a myriad of physical, mental, emotional, and spiritual issues. In my opinion, most, if not all, issues stem from hara line distortions and misalignment since the chakras also lay on this major pathway.

Pranic Tube Meditation

Sit or stand so that your spine is erect, and you feel comfortable. Begin to breathe into your hara line and heart until you feel calm and present. Imagine that there is a shining, golden-white star far above your head. This will symbolize your Source, God/Goddess/All That Is.

Invite and imagine that a flowing stream of energy flows down from Source and passes through your crown, all the way through the body, and down into the Earth. Breath this Source Light into your Hara, into your womb, filling it with pure, clear, golden-white energy. Exhale and send the energy down into the Earth. Repeat this breathing pattern a few times and allow this pure Source Energy to sweep away any stagnant or dense energy and release it down into the Earth to be composted. This will not harm the planet. She lovingly takes all our sorrows and struggles and transforms them for us.

Bring your hands onto your heart and feel your own heart's energy. Breathe into it and help it shine. Intend to sense Gaia's heart. Intend to connect to her pulsating rhythm of love. Begin to breathe her love and evolutionary coding up through your hara line into your own heart. Fill your heart with this love and as you exhale, send this love back to Source. Continue a few more times, breathing all this love up into the body and feel Gaia's heart, your heart, and the heart of Creation flowing together and synchronizing.

Bring your hands down to your lap and breathe normally. Sense what has shifted and enjoy your moment. When you are finished, feel blessed to have this connection and open your eyes.

Pranic Tube Tune-Up and Boundaries

Throughout the day, you can clear out your hara line and realign with your Divine Purpose. Simply use conscious breathing, intention, and imagination. As you inhale, bring the energy down from Source into your hara channeling down the Divine Presence, then exhale, grounding the energy into Gaia. Inhale drawing earth energy up from the core of Gaia into your heart. Exhale, send the energy back to Source fully establishing the bridge. Inhale from Gaia and Source, then exhale, radiating light outward, re-establishing your field's boundaries. Make your entire "breathing space" illuminated with compassionate presence. Repeat the pattern until you reach the desired state of stability, peace, and wholeness. In just three breath cycles, you can completely refresh and revitalize your entire energy system and your consciousness and avoid unnecessary suffering.

Nadis

Nadis, Sanskrit for "river channel," are pathways for our subtle energy to move throughout our bioelectric system. The physical manifestation of the nadis include the nerves and fascial grid. Some ancient texts say that there are over 72,000 nadis that weave a matrix of light around and within your body that lead to every cell of your physicality. The three major nadis as called *ida*, *pingala*, and *sushumna*.

Ida and Pingala

Ida and *pingala nadis*, related to the vagus nerves, represent the feminine and masculine polarities of our personality. These two serpent energies weave through our chakra system to create conduits of consciousness that meet in the Brow Center. These two energy pathways play such an important role in health and wellness that the symbol of the *caduceus* has been used by the medical/healing world for a long time. This symbol is depicted as the wand that Hermes or Mercury carries in Greek and Roman mythology.

Ida nadi, the feminine pathway, starts in the root chakra on the left and weaves its way up through the chakras finishing at our left nostril at the brow center. Often associated with the moon, this feminine energy is considered reflective, intuitive, cooling, and nurturing and is described as the mental force, *manas shakti*. This current is active when the left nostril is flowing, and the right hemisphere of the brain is active.

Pingala nadi, the masculine pathway, begins at the root chakra on the right and weaves its way up through the chakras finishing at the right nostril at the brow center. Often associated with solar qualities, this masculine power directs life force energy, *prana shakti*, to energize all essential life processes and is related to heat, logic, assertiveness, and action. This current is active when the right nostril is flowing, and the left-brain hemisphere is activated.

As we breathe in and out through our nose, air carries subtle energy through these two pathways to clear and revitalize the chakra system. As we switch between our consciousness's masculine and feminine qualities, one or the other pathways become dominant. Although without balance and awareness, we can either overstress our energy systems or become lethargic.

The most direct and transformative way I know to balance the masculine and feminine qualities of our consciousness is through the alternate nostril breathing technique, *nadi shodhanam,* and the system of hatha yoga. That being said, all effective healing and personal transformational processes inherently involve the balancing of these polarities.

Sushumna Nadi and Kundalini Shakti

The *sushumna* is the part of our hara line related to our physical body and the seven-chakra system. This tube of light charges and energizes the chakra system. It runs from the base of the spine at the perineum up to the crown of the head. At the base of the *sushumna,* wrapped around the base of the spine, lies the *kundalini shakti,* the ecstatic expression and spiritual potential of your spiritual being.

The *kundalini* energy is said to sit coiled at the base of the spine in *muladhara chakra,* the Root Center. As a soul progresses through incarnations, certain interactions begin to activate this dormant energy and it begins to rise up through *sushumna* balancing the polarities of each chakra as it makes its upward ascension. These two polarities eventually join at the Brow Center to create an experience that some call *Hieros Gamos,* which refers to this alchemical unification of the twin flame polarities within which is the goal of *hatha yoga* practices. Once this has occurred, *kundalini* can make its full ascension to the Crown Center to create the experience called *moksha, nirvana,* salvation, or any of the other names which describe fully realized Godself Consciousness.

Kundalini awakening can be felt like a surge of electrical current from the root of the spine into the higher energy centers of the brow and crown chakras. This can be experienced with body tremors, waves of wisdom and insight, waves of ecstasy, spontaneous mudras and positionings of the body, big emotional shifts, visionary experiences, sensory overload, and more.

Kundalini shakti, the ecstatic, spiritual potential within one's consciousness, begins to rise up the spine and activate each chakra and balance the consciousness at each center on its ascension towards the crown. For most people, *kundalini* rises and then goes back to rest in the Root Center while the practitioner reconciles their consciousness. Progress in one life carries over to the next life. Many "spiritual people" or those on the awakening path have had *kundalini* activation in previous lives and will continue this lifetime working in the chakra that they left off with in the "previous" incarnation. It is said that most of those on the "spiritual path" have at least activated the first three chakras and are beginning to work towards the heart chakra.

As humanity ascends, the awakening of the serpent energies can be quite powerful and intoxicating. As we heal and integrate our consciousness's masculine and feminine qualities, we awaken and stir our creative, sexual-spiritual energies. It is important to learn practices of grounding to work with these energies effectively and safely.

Ascension alchemy practices like Ancient Egyptian sex magic, true tantra, and kundalini and hatha yoga are designed to awaken these energy systems, purify them, and unify our consciousness with the Absolute. While it can be intoxicating and exhilarating to stay in states of kundalini activation, it is also important to ingest foods and participate in activities that nourish and soothe our nervous systems so that we do not "burn out" or overstress them. I recommend seeking out a teacher or a guide who can safely guide you through kundalini awakening if you are feeling unstable through your awakening process.

Chakras: Lenses to See the World

Emerging from *sushumna* channel, we have the blooming of seven main energy vortexes commonly known as the "*chakras.*" The chakra system goes by different names in different traditions. These seals/wheels/lamps/vortices tether our physical body with our subtle body processes. They are toroidal in shape and always in states of movement and evolution. They contain life force energy as well as mental energy. Like individual minds, each contains our programmed beliefs about the seven major areas of our life, such as community and physical life, self-identity and relationships, willpower, compassion, communication, vision, and universality. Besides the seven main chakras, there are many sub-chakras and micro-chakras throughout the body with some existing outside of the body. However, these seven are the most important when cultivating consciousness liberation and holistic wellness.

Each of the seven main chakras relates to certain glands in the endocrine system, nerve plexi, and particular organs and bodily systems. As energy information passes through the aura, it is processed through the chakra system and creates emotional/mental/physical experiences based on our beliefs and previous experiences with similar dynamics. This energy ripples out across the subtle energy pathways (nadis/meridians) into the nervous system and endocrine system to create sensations, bodily functions, and events.

Chakra Locations

Here are the locations of the seven main chakras, the two minor chakras, and the three newly emerging ascension chakras:

- **Soul Star Center:** Felt 6-12 inches above the head
- **Crown Center:** Crown of the head
- **Brow Center:** Between the forehead and occiput
- **Zeal Center:** Emanating from the medulla oblongata, attachment point of the spine to the skull
- **Throat Center:** Center of the throat
- **Heart Center:** Felt between and behind the manubrium and xiphoid process of the sternum
- **Solar Plexus Center:** Just below the diaphragm
- **Sacral Center:** Low abdomen behind the naval
- **Root Center:** Base of the spine at the pelvic floor
- **Earth Star Center:** Below the feet when standing, below the pelvis when seated
- **Palm Chakras:** Center of the palms
- **Foot Chakras:** Soles of the feet

Chakra Filaments: How We Feel Our Environment

Chakras radiate filaments of light, just like the rays and filaments of the sun. The number of filaments on a chakra relates to the frequency of the chakra. The higher the frequency, the higher the number of petals opening from the electromagnetic flower.

These filaments reach out to interact with a specific layer of our auric field. Picture a plasma ball from science class with the violet plasma whipping across the inside of the glass globe. Each filament reaches through its environment to absorb the energy information in the world around us while simultaneously broadcasting our essence into the field. The chakras respond to our attention. As we focus our energy on an object, they begin to drink in the energy of the object of our attention.

Attachments and Cords

When we develop an attachment to an object, our energy forms a habit of focusing on the object of our attention. Unhealthy relationships are a result of unhealthy beliefs and a habit of attaching our energy to the object. They are habits of where we direct our life force. Cords develop between people that relate in unhealthy ways, thus creating codependent patterns.

To reconcile this once you become aware of an unhealthy relationship, practice the Hara Line Aura Meditation and return to sovereign alignment with the Source Within You. To create permanent change, you can work on identifying and shifting your belief systems that caused the unhealthy patterns, or they will return later until you fully see and heal this part of your subconscious.

Distortion in Our Subtle Bodies

Even before we are born, we begin to absorb the mental patterning of the world beyond our mother's womb. Some people experience trauma within the womb and carry it throughout their life. Additionally, our DNA is filled with energy information from the lifetimes of those who came before us who passed down the genetic coding through our lineages. As mentioned before, life experiences also reactivate stored information in our causal body that brings forth patterns created in past lives.

Traumatic life experiences, memories, and energies often get trapped in all layers of the bodymind complex. Slowly over time, they release so that we do not feel the full brunt of the psychophysical trauma at the moment of the event. When energy is not reconciled, the bodymind tries to release the energy in some way. This can look like crying, sighing, shaking, screaming, sleeping, illness, dreams, and so on. If we practice meditation and self-healing, we can speed up our recovery process significantly.

If we suppress or ignore our emotions and trapped energy, the negative effects begin to show up in our physical bodies. Over time patterns begin to crystallize and become more physical as the bodymind tries to eliminate the distorted energy information. From the most subtle inflammation to the most aggressive cancer, it all has its roots in the subtle energy system. We can use our conscious awareness to reconcile traumatic injuries in our bodies and return to wholeness and vitality.

The *chakras* are constantly broadcasting our internal world and magnetizing events to them that reflect the stored subconscious beliefs. The distortions and trauma stored within our subconscious show up in our life as manifestations of similar circumstances that trigger the trauma patterning. This "clashing" brings our unconscious patterns to the surface so that we can exhaust and potentially integrate the energy information from the past experience and grow in consciousness maturity. From this perspective, we can understand how we create our reality and how everything truly begins within our very own consciousness. As within, so without.

With conscious awareness and subtle energy healing techniques, you can unpack the information stored within the emotions, thought patterns, and physical body events and reconcile the energy. This naturally brings a deeper understanding, and wisdom is revealed through the healing process. This frees up the pathways so that energy can flow freely, and we experience a more joyful, conscious life.

Illness and disease are the body's intelligence giving us a massive wake-up call to tune into our inner being and create a rich, inner life that is luminous and vital. As we tune into subtle energy, we unlock the mysteries of the bodymind's intelligence and begin to accelerate in consciousness growth and authentic empowerment.

Pranayama: Entering the Dimension of Prana

Breathing is one of the main ways that we regulate the movement of the life force in the body. Each inhalation brings in fresh, new life force energy to be used by the body's cells and systems. Each exhalation expels old stagnant energy that is no longer needed by the body. One of the secrets to living a long and vibrant life is the power of conscious breathing.

Breath cycles are made of four stages. *Puraka*, a deep, rich inhalation, focuses the mind and energizes the cells and systems of the body. Inner breath retention, *antar kumbhaka*, equally distributes, calms, and clarifies prana. Conscious exhalation, *rechaka*, releases toxins and calms the bodymind. External breath retention, *bahya kumbhaka*, moves *prana* up the spine to the brain and creates a sense of non-attachment, peace, and inner silence. Women who are pregnant and people with high blood pressure, lung, heart, eye, or ear problems should not hold either phase of breath retention. Instead, they should focus only on the inhalation and exhalations.

Below is a descriptive list of breathing practices, called *pranayama* by the ancient yogis, to get you started with the basics. When you first begin practicing *pranayama*, start with learning to equalize the duration of the inhalation and exhalations in a 1:1 ratio (using a count of four or five seconds) with a slight pause in between inhalation and exhalation. Then increase exhalation duration by doubling the number in a 1:2 ratio. Once this is mastered, add in inhalation breath retention for a ratio of 1:2:2. For more advanced practices, I recommend checking out the *Hatha Yoga Pradipika*.

As you do these practices, keep an easy mind and relaxed body while sitting in a tall, meditative posture. If at any point you feel frustration or tension, stop the practice, return to neutral, and start again when you are ready.

Another practice that I highly recommend is the use of a *neti* pot which looks somewhat like a tea pot and is used for a sinus washing process that clears obstructions out of the nasal passageway. This practice called *jala neti* will increase the body's absorption of prana during breathing and help to awaken subtle consciousness in the brow center.

Three-Part Breathing or Yogic Breathing (Dirga Pranayam)

This breathing style incorporates the full range of breathing capacity utilizing abdominal, thoracic, and clavicular breathing awareness. This practice oxygenates and nourishes the whole body and is great for reducing anxiety and stress.

First, exhale completely until you feel the lower abdomen contract and the pelvic floor lift. Softly release the lower abdomen and allow it to expand with your inhale. After the abdomen expands, allow the chest to expand, feel the energy of the inhale rise up through your spine and into the crown of your head. Softly exhale and reverse the process and allow the air and energy to drain down from the head, softening the chest, exhaling completely until the lower abdomen contracts and the pelvic floor lifts. Repeat, softly extending each segment of the cycle of breath. As you do this, you can imagine that you are surrounded by brilliant, clear, white light. With each breath, you can breathe this fresh light into all the cells of the body.

Samma Vritti: Equal Flow Box Breath

This breathing practice is called "box breath" as the patterning can be thought of as the equal dimensions of a square with inhalation, breath retention after inhalation, exhalation, and breath retention after exhalation. Start simply with a count of four during each stage. Then you can increase the number as you develop control and calmness of the bodymind within each stage. This can be done with regular yogic breathing as well as in alternate nostril breathing.

Kapalbhati: Skull-Cleansing Breath

This breathing practice gets its name because of its revitalizing and healing properties. *Kapalbhati* clears the mind, burns away stagnant energy, clears the respiratory system, and brightens the face and higher chakras. In this practice, inhalations are relaxed, and deep and rapid force is applied to the exhale.

Pregnant or menstruating women should not do this practice nor should people with spinal injuries. If you have high blood pressure, stomach ulcers, or any other health issues, be gentle (one pump per second) until you see how the body works with the practice.

Using the three-part breathing, inhale fully and allow the belly and chest to fill with air. On the exhale, contract the abdomen strongly back towards the spine, feeling a strong pulse of air exit the nose. Softly relax the abdomen and allow the lungs to fill with air. Repeat this pattern, slowly increasing the cycles' speed, creating a rapid breathing pattern that is also relaxed in mind and emotions.

Repeat for around twenty to thirty rounds. On the last exhale, gently push out all the excess air until you feel the pelvic floor and abdomen contract. Drop the chin towards the chest and gently lift the heart towards the chin to make an energetic lock. Hold for a few moments, then release the head and soften the throat, abdomen, and pelvic floor. Find a neutral position of the spine and return to normal conscious breathing and observe your internal experience. If it feels right, you can add consecutive rounds of practice.

Bhastrika: Bellows Breath

Bellows Breath energizes the mind and body, tones the abdominal muscles, and builds the digestive fire. This is a great practice to do if you are feeling tired, confused, or sluggish. It focuses on equal force of inhales and exhales. The practice is often done with arm movement to help with the expansion and contraction of the lungs.

Sit comfortably and find your natural, three-part breathing. After a complete exhale, bring your arms up above your head, spreading the fingers wide as you reach for the sky, and inhale deeply with gentle force. Exhale by strongly contracting the abdomen towards the spine while simultaneously closing the fingers into fists and pulling the elbow down towards the ribs, contracting the muscles of your arms and abdomen fully as you exhale. Inhale deeply to raise the arms back up above the head and repeat the cycle for twenty to thirty rounds. After you exhale, bring the arms down, rest the hands on the legs or ground, and observe your inner experience. If desired, you can repeat the practice.

Bhramari Breath: Bee Breath

Bhramari Breath uses breath and toning of the vocal cords to send vibrations through the throat and skull. The long exhalations assist the autonomic nervous system by inducing a relaxation response through the lengthened exhales. This practice is excellent for anyone who needs to calm the mind and focus their intention.

Sit comfortably in your meditation posture and do several rounds of full yogic breathing. Raise both hands in front of the face with your elbows pointing outwards, in line with the shoulders, with the palms facing you. Close your eyes, gently press the index fingers to the inner corners of the eyes, place the middle fingers on either side of the nose, the ring fingers above the lips, and the little fingers below the mouth. Use the thumbs to gently close the ears.

Another option is to take your hands and rub them together, activating them with light and energy. Bring the hands up to each side of the head, blocking the ears by pressing lightly on the tragus of each ear to close the ear canal. Take the other fingers and lightly touch the brow with the pads of the fingers. Fingers should be spread across the forehead and hairline.

Once your hand position is set you can begin the "bee's breath." At the top of the inhale, begin to make a humming sound with the lips closed. Draw out the sound and play with the pitch of the tones. Feel the vibrations moving throughout your nostrils, sinuses, throat, and brain. Imagine that your hands' vibrations and energy pulsations are breaking apart unhealthy thought patterns and upgrading the neural pathways. Fill the skull and throat with vibrations. Do this for about six rounds. Then drop the mudra and sound and feel the subtle shifts happening along the pathways of energy.

Nadi Shodhanam: Alternate Nostril Breathing

Alternate nostril breathing balances the right and left hemispheres of the brain and the masculine and feminine principles of consciousness, creating a state of calm focus. This practice is especially useful when you feel anxiety or stress. It is a wonderful practice to do before you start anything that needs your full attention and awareness. There are a variety of methods to do alternate nostril breathing. Here is a basic practice:

Take the index and middle fingers of the right hand and lightly touch the center of the brow. You will be using the inside of the ring finger and the pad of the thumb to block and alternate the passage of air through the nostrils. The other hand can be resting on your lap, in jnana mudra, resting on your heart, or in any other comfortable position.

Using the thumb, gently press against the outside of the nose to close the right nostril and exhale completely through the left nostril, gently contracting the lower abdomen and pelvic floor at the bottom of the exhale. Then breathe in through the left nostril as you release the abdominal contraction. Feel the air and energy circulating in the center of the brow under the fingertips. Gently pause at the top without adding tension to the face or upper torso.

Switch nostrils, block the left nostril with the inside of the ring finger, release the thumb off the right nostril, and exhale through the right nostril until you feel the abdomen and pelvic floor contract. Pause for a moment. Then breathe in through the right nostril feeling the air circulate at the brow. Pause again.

Close the right nostril, open the left nostril, and exhale through the left until you feel the abdominal and pelvic floor contractions.

Repeat for at least two to three minutes or longer. Meditate on smoothing out and evening each segment of the breath. A suggestion of ratio would be to start first with a 1:1 ratio, building up to 1:2.

Combined Practice Suggestion:

- 3 rounds kapalbhati (30-50 pulses per round)
- 2 rounds of Bhastrika (30-50 pulses per round)
- 3 complete breaths (natural breathing)
- 3 rounds of nadi shodhanam (2-3 minutes per round)
- 2-3 minutes of bhramari
- Breath awareness
- Meditation

For a shorter practice, you can skip the *bhastrika* breath and keep the cleansing benefits of *kapalbhati.*

Circular Breathing

This breathing practice goes by many names, some of which are trademarked. This type of breathwork involves deep, continuous breathing cycles that highly oxygenate the body and reduce carbon dioxide. This circular breathing pattern is known to help reduce depression, process and integrate trauma, eliminate fears and phobias, and much more. It is known to induce altered states of consciousness and awaken unconscious memory for processing and integration. Many people report having psychedelic-like experiences. It is not recommended to do this practice if you have cardiac or respiratory health issues. Go gentle at first and see how you respond, then you can decide whether to increase or reduce the intensity or duration of the practice. It is recommended to do these practices with a trained facilitator who can guide you through emotional experiences, involuntary muscle spasms, or other powerful experiences. If you are doing this practice alone, go gently and feel it out.

1. Lay down on a flat and comfortable surface. You may wish to cover yourself with a blanket. Keep the head flat on the ground, no pillow, so that the spine stays long and even.
2. Start with a progressive relaxation body scan.
3. Begin the circular breathing pattern with deep inhalations and deep exhalations, no pausing in between. Try to make it seamless.
4. Be careful not to push or strain the body. Back off the edge a bit.
5. Pick up the speed. Do it a little faster than normal but not so fast that the body tenses.
6. It is perfectly normal and common for the face muscles or the hands or feet to contract. Keep breathing through it, nice and gently.
7. If fear or other powerful emotions arise, breathe through them. You can back off the intensity a bit if you wish.
8. Do the practice for about 10-20 minutes. Then relax completely and feel the effects for another 10 minutes or so.

The Microcosmic Orbit

The microcosmic orbit circulates life force throughout the entire system of the body. Sit mindfully and quiet the mind by bringing your awareness to your breath. Bring the tongue to touch the back of the teeth and roof of the mouth to close the "heavenly gate" and gently lift the pelvic floor to close the "earthly gate." This creates an energetic loop that connects the front and back of the body. Breathe mindfully into the pelvis and imagine that the pelvic bowl is filling with white light. As you inhale, sweep the white light towards your sacrum and up your spine, cresting at the top of the head. As you exhale, sweep the white light down the front of your face and body and back to your pelvis. Continue circulating your awareness, breath, and the white light through this orbit until you feel clear, clean, and balanced in your energy. When you are finished, simply return to regular conscious breathing, and observe your Inner Being's sensations.

Pranic Body Summary

We are a bridge between the higher consciousness realms and Earth, existing in an ever-changing matrix of subtle energy. We access this connection through our hara line and personal energy field. As energy information passes through our energy field, it is dispersed to energy vortexes called chakras, transforming the data through our belief center programming, creating emotions. Emotions pulse out a charge of energy that fractals out along the nadis/meridians to create physical body processes and our perception of ourselves and the world around us. We can use the power of our breathing and breath awareness to reconcile our consciousness and return all systems to health and balance. As we raise our vibration and awareness, we move beyond the need for illness and disease as a teacher of karma and move into the perfection of our Divine Blueprint as conscious embodiments of the Breath of Life.

NINE

Postures for Channeling Light

Mudra is a Sanskrit word for energy locks. They are different ways to posture the body to affect the flow of subtle energy. Different traditions have different ways of holding hands to shift subtle energy. If you know any of them and their effects, you can use those when channeling Light. Otherwise, use your intuition. You may have already noticed that the body subconsciously moves the fingers into certain placements at different times throughout the day. This is especially true for those who have studied healing and the Mysteries in other lifetimes. The subconscious remembers the training and guides the body into postures to open the flow of energy and healing.

When we use the power of mudras, we open our body temple instrument to be an oracle for Divine Consciousness. Mudras are keys to unlocking pathways to meet the energy that is being evoked to channel. When we create a mudra and intend to connect with the Light, our biofield and etheric structures rearrange to allow the Divine Frequency Transmission. This sends waves of Light emanating from the entire body temple out into the field.

As we move about the Earth, we can consciously transmit divine frequencies into the field around us. Our bodies are bio-transducers, constantly absorbing energy from the environment and transmuting it through our body systems. As conscious beings, we can support the collective ascension process by channeling divine love into the Earth Reality.

When you consciously tune into Source Energy and the life force of Gaia, you naturally stand tall with an open chest. You beam loving energy through your entire being, bridging Heaven and Earth. You can beam Truth and Oneness out into the world through your gaze and broadcast light from your hands as you breathe consciously.

I will describe some hand *mudra*s and their possible psychospiritual effects. Although each person will experience the power of these hand positions in their own way, I describe specific hand gestures for different mudras. Experiment with the opposite hand as well and discover your own experience with the hand's placements.

Take a few minutes to try each of these hand placements and postures to feel their subtle energy and consciousness effects. If any of them feel uncomfortable or if you notice unpleasant shifts or changes happening after practicing the mudra, stop working with that mudra. A full list of contraindications for each mudra can be found online or in texts dedicated to the various effects of mudras.

Anjali-Gassho: Prayer Hands Mudra

This mudra is made with both palms together in a prayer position with the thumbs touching the Heart Center. This mudra is used by many spiritual and religious cultures around the world and back through antiquity. This mudra unites the right and left sides of the brain and closes our auric field. It connects us with our divinity and to the power of the heart-mind.

Gyan/Jnana Mudra: Knowledge Mudra

This mudra is made by connecting the index and thumb fingertips and extending the middle, ring, and pinky fingers creating the hand symbol of OK. It is also commonly accepted to do it with the tip of the index finger touching the base of the top knuckle of the thumb. This seal is considered the mudra of Knowledge. It focuses the mind on peace, higher intelligence, and wisdom. When the same mudra is made with the palms facing down it is called *chin mudra* (consciousness mudra) and evokes a feeling of groundedness and concentration. Both are excellent for meditation.

Dhyana Mudra: Meditation Mudra

This mudra is made with the right hand holding the left hand. Allow the thumbs to connect to create a triangular circuit of energy. This mudra connects and unifies the body, mind, and soul through the heart field. It charges our central channel and connects us with the prayerful beings and enlightened masters of the Earth and beyond.

Bhairava Mudra: Fierce Mudra

This mudra is made with the left hand resting in the lap while the right hand rests on top. This symbolizes the masculine (right side) resting into the feminine (left side), creating a harmonious feeling (enhances *pingala*). When reversed with the right holding the left, the masculine energy supports the divine feminine energy for awakening and manifestation (enhancing *ida nadi*). It is said to eliminate negative effects of ego and illness.

Varada Mudra: Bestower of Boons Mudra

Associated with the sharing of blessings, mercy, and love, this mudra is made with the right or left hand with the palm facing forward and the fingers pointing down. I typically place this mudra along the right side of my body below the level of my naval. For me, this mudra generates a peaceful, grounding energy that blesses the field around me.

Abhaya Mudra: Courage/Fearlessness Mudra

This mudra is made with the right hand to the side of the body level with the heart. The palm is facing forward with the fingertips pointing toward the heavens. This mudra evokes peace, dispels fear, and welcomes the protection and presence of the Divine.

Abhaya & Varada Mudras: Blessings & Courage

Combine both mudras using the right (upward) and left (downward) hands to bridge the blessed energies of Earth and Sky. Feel the combined energies of grounded peace and the higher frequencies of the higher realms.

Prana Mudra: Life Force Mudra

This mudra is made with the right hand with the pinky, ring finger, and thumb touching. The peace fingers and index and middle fingers are extended upwards and connected. This mudra activates the flow of prana and the root chakra's grounding power, creating a powerful energy transmission.

Prithvi Mudra: Assimilation Mudra

This mudra is made with the right thumb and ring finger touching, with the peace fingers and pinky extended. This "Seal of Life" creates stability by strengthening and healing the physical body. This balances the earth and fire elements of the body and is powerful for healing many ailments.

Ardhapataka Mudra: Half-Flag Mudra

This mudra is made with the thumb, index, and middle fingers extended while the ring and pinky fingers are bent towards the palm. This "sign of benediction" bestows blessings and frees the consciousness of nuisance and disturbance.

Karana Mudra: Purification Mudra

The mudra is made by pressing the pad of the thumb over the nail of the middle finger with the other fingers extended. The ring finger will likely be bent a bit. This mudra "dispels darkness" by clearing obstacles and challenges on the path of awakening and Ascension.

Intent Mudra

This mudra is made by bringing the palms together in a prayer position in front of the solar plexus with wrists touching the solar plexus and the fingers pointing out away from the body. Right thumb crosses over the left to make a circuit. Space between the palms with fingertips touching. This is a wonderful mudra to do whenever you want to cultivate willpower and strength.

Whole Body Transmission

Bring soft tension into your arms and hands and intend for healing energy to flow through them. Tune into your hara line and your loving connection to Source and Gaia. Turn the palms in the direction that you wish to direct the energy.

While you do this, broadcast Love and Light through your Brow Center in the direction of the person, place, or object you hope to illuminate. Feel radiant and filled with Unconditional Love and Unity. Beam undulating waves of love from your heart. Beam dazzling rainbow light from your entire being and completely fill the space with light. Finish with a blessing and dedication, said out loud or internally, "May all beings be free. May all beings know love."

Heart Beacon

Bring your nondominant hand to your heart and intend to connect with your inner Light. Form the other hand in *abhaya mudra* to hold light and shine it into the world around you. If you want the energy to be a higher frequency, have the palm facing outward, in line with the heart or higher, with the fingers pointing upward. For more subtle and grounded heart energy, have the palm down by the side, fingers pointing down towards the Earth in *varada mudra*.

Creative Beacon

Bring your nondominant hand to touch upon your sacral center/lower abdomen/womb space. Feel your connection to Source and Gaia. With the palm pointing outward and fingertips pointing downward or to the side, beam creative and grounding energies into the space. As you create the energies within yourself, they flow out of your field and into the space.

High Calling

Bring the arms up to the heavens to call in Divine Light from Source. Feel your hara line and breathe into it. This is a powerful pose that will generate a powerful feeling.

Earth Field Awakening

Bow down and place your hands upon the Earth to connect to the planetary grid. Slowly begin to stand and use your intention and movement of your arms to raise up frequencies of Light from within the Earth. I often use the imagery of calling up cities of light and illumined beings from Earth's Light realms. Use this connection to make a dance that awakens the radiant energies of Gaia in your awareness.

Spinning Vortex of Light

Imagine that you are connected to Source and Gaia through a bright pillar of clear light. Spin the body in a clockwise rotation with the arms raised out and imagine that you are spreading light in infinite directions. This will naturally clear your auric field and send beautiful light all around you. Come to stillness slowly. Ground down through your legs. Bring one hand to your heart and one hand to your hara and feel the powerful vortex you have created.

If you would like to learn more about the power of the hands for healing, I suggest studying the sections dedicated to the art of the Laying of Hands.

TEN

Ascension Symptom Care

Lightbody ascension practices are found in many ancient cultures, especially in India, Tibet, and Ancient Egypt. The systems focus on transformation by refining the physical, vital, emotional, mental, intuitional, intellectual, and spiritual bodies so that a being embodies Divine Light and their Divine I AM Presence. As we clear our lower energies, we make way for the Light of the Higher Realms to descend into our physical vessel so that we radiate Light and Truth out into the world.

In the past, once an initiate reached a high enough vibration and the highest level of enlightenment they could reach in the body, they would consciously shed the body to continue learning in the higher realms in their Lightbody. Sometimes they would go into a trance and consciously leave the body, or some highly advanced initiates who could control the frequency of their cells would spin them faster and faster until they shifted beyond the visible light spectrum into the higher realms as their physical body dissolved into thin air. Yeshua ben Joseph (Jesus) made this ascension process popular, but it has also been documented and written about by other cultures, especially the Egyptians and Tibetan Buddhists.

What is different about our upcoming ascension is that we will be transforming our physical body into a lighter form and taking it with us into the next dimension of consciousness and reality. What was once only available to select initiates through arduous purification and healing practices in secluded temples and monasteries is now available to all people committed to compassionate heart-based living and have done the work to raise their overall vibration.

As we prepare for Gaia's transformation from Third Density Earth to Fourth Density Gaia, our DNA is being restored back to the Adamic form, the original pristine human Lightbody. Many alterations have been made to the human DNA throughout humanity's time on Earth, and we are in a purging process of all the distortions stored within our multidimensional genetic structure and sequencing.

These distortions are the product of genetic implantation from other star races, ancestral memory, mental fields absorbed from the collective thought patterns, toxicity from our environments, damage from the cataclysm of Atlantis, and more. As these ascension energies move through our system, they clear any blockages we have accrued so that we can hold more light. This can appear as cold/flu-like symptoms, increased body heat, heightened intuition, foggy mind, dizziness, chest pain, digestive issues, vivid dreams, emotional purging, paranormal experiences, ringing in the ears, dehydration, and more.

Below is a list of guidelines to support the ascension and Lightbody activation and recalibration processes. This is not meant to be "medical advice" but speaks to common experiences held by myself and others in the global ascension community.

If you feel that you are unhealthy and at risk for serious health concerns, please see a medical professional. I highly recommend seeing a medical professional who treats clients holistically. Western medicine is trained to focus on symptoms. Eastern medicine and holistic healthcare professionals are trained to look for root causes and treat entire systems to bring the body back into homeostasis.

Meditation: Calling in Light

Meditation is a crucial step in this process. Developing self-awareness helps you discern what is best for your path so that you can release what no longer serves you. Meditation practices that utilize conscious breathing are some of the best tools to ground your energy, clear out stagnant energy, and revitalize your personal energy field as fresh life force enters through the breath. Visualizing clear, bright light moving through the body helps raise the body's vibration and transform dense energy into a more refined and clear energy signature. Let the sunshine in!

Dehydration

Many health problems stem from chronic dehydration. Drink plenty of fresh spring water to hydrate the tissues and cells of the body. Municipal water sources often contain chlorine, fluoride, or other chemicals that poison our bodies and mind. Adding trace-mineral hydration salts to your water helps the water absorb into the cells. Also, consider taking a "cell salt" supplement to support healthy cellular function. Adding magnesium to your hydration practice will also help with discomfort in the chest/heart region when assimilating the energies. This will also help with headaches and anxious feelings.

Silica Supplements

It has been recommended that we all take silica supplements to support our body's transition from being carbon-based to a crystalline, silica-based Lightbody. This will help with achy joints, cognitive functioning, and more.

Essential Oils and Plant Medicine

Nature knows best. Herbs and plant extracts work with our body's cells and consciousness to bring our systems into homeostasis. This includes medicines like psylocibin, cannabis, hemp, kava, and other plant allies to help us soothe the ascension process and connect with higher intelligence for healing and transformation. Of course, intention and safety are important for all medicine journeys. Keep it sacred!

High-quality essential oils that are certified pure and organic safely work with the body's cells to support the body's natural ability to heal itself. Some oils can be taken internally, and most are safe for topical and aromatic use. Check with each oil's health and protocol guidelines to understand how to use the oil safely and properly.

When using topically, consider using a vegetable/nut-based carrier oil to help spread the essential oil across the skin. If an essential oil is applied topically and causes irritation, dilute and clean with a carrier oil. Do not use water as this drives the essential oil further into the tissue.

Detoxify the Body

Physical symptoms include a variety of detoxification symptoms as toxins are released from the body. You may notice a diet change as the body craves fresh, organic fruits and vegetables and less meat. There will not be meat or killing of any kind when we shift to the New Earth consciousness.

Everyone should follow their own guidance about what nourishment their body needs at any given time. Periodic fasting can help the elimination process as well as eating a naturally detoxifying diet. Eating fresh greens fills the body systems with biophotons, light particles to support healthy system functionality. Switch to natural, organic products versus products with toxic chemical ingredients to reduce your organs' toxic load. You may feel guided to do a cleanse regimen like a liver cleanse or kidney cleanse, or a heavy metal detox to help the body eliminate toxins.

Cellular Oxidation

Radiation from cosmic energies, solar events, 5G radiation, and other energies puts stress on our body's cells. Increase antioxidant intake and supplements that promote cellular health and reverse the effects of oxidative stress.

Alkalize the Body

Reduce the body's acidity to reduce inflammation and support the body's natural ability to heal itself. This includes eating a mostly "sattvic" diet or a "yogic diet" which is simple and free from processed ingredients and synthetics. Practices like drinking apple cider vinegar, fresh lemon juice, or citrus essential oils help to break apart and eliminate toxic build-up in the body.

Detoxify People, Places, and Things

Spend less and less time around people that are vexatious to your system. Find like-minded people who are loving and gentle to spend your time with. Avoid places with highly charged energies when you are feeling extra sensitive. Many find that they need to spend more quality time alone or with their pets and limit their social interactions to focus on their own healing and expansion. Declutter your home to free up stagnant energy. As within, so without!

Rest and Sleep

Listen to the body and honor when it is asking for rest. At times, the body will need much more rest and sleep as it adjusts to the shifting frequencies. Sometimes, you may not be able to sleep because of the rush of plasma entering your field from the ascension energies. Be gentle with yourself. Natural sleep aids, teas, and herbal supplements help the body stay in deeper sleep to feel refreshed when you awaken. Chamomile and lavender can help you prepare for a deep night's rest.

Get Into Nature

Nature has a grounding and centering effect on our consciousness and nervous system. Take frequent trips into nature away from people, pollution, and technology. "Earthing" or walking barefoot on the ground helps to ground pent-up energy in your nervous system, leaving you feeling grounded and clear. If you cannot stand on soil, you can stand on a layer of sea salt to ground your energy. Use a container to stand in so that you do not make a mess!

Ringing in the Ears

The electromagnetic fields of the Earth and the planetary grid will be unstable in the process, as will our own energetic field. The ringing of the ears is common for people at different times as waves of plasma enter the Earth. Some people find themselves to be extra sensitive to Electromagnetic Frequencies (EMFs). Many devices and crystals (e.g., shungite) are available to help reduce the negative effects of EMFs on the body and consciousness. It is suggested that we take as much time as we can to get off our devices, out of range of Wi-Fi and cell towers, and immerse ourselves in the regenerative field of Nature. Return to the wild and wonderful!

Headaches, Dizziness, and Cognitive Functioning

These energies affect our minds as we shed lower beliefs and upgrade the brain's anatomy and cognitive functioning. This could manifest as states of confusion and feeling sensations in the brain, including headaches, energy movement, and pulsations.

Dizziness and headaches can be a sign that you need more water and need to ground excess energy. Consciously ground the energy through intention and meditative practices or walk barefoot on the earth. Increase water intake and rest until the dizziness subsides. Add hydration salts, trace minerals, cellular salts, and silica supplements to support the process. Essential oils like peppermint and lavender help soothe head and neck tension to alleviate pressure in the head.

Digestive System Issues

The digestive system not only processes food to create energy, but the solar plexus digests subtle energy for a variety of processes. Many find that their digestive system is either over or underactive at different times. I recommend using a natural digestive supplement, digestive enzyme supplement, or laying of hands to support the healing process. Essential oils like ginger and peppermint help support healthy digestive processes.

Low Energy and Fatigue

Sometimes, no matter how much you rest, it may not feel like enough. Using invigorating essential oils can boost the mood and increase focus. There are many natural food supplements to use to boost energy like cacao, maca, and spirulina. If you use caffeine, I suggest using tea, especially yerba mate, versus coffee to reduce acidity in the body. Essential oils like peppermint and citrus oils help to lift the mood and focus the mind.

Soaking in Water

Water is a powerful tool to use to ground and clear energy. Find natural sources of water to swim in or soak your feet. Take baths with natural salts and minerals added to the water to help clear and restore. Adding your favorite essential oils, candles, and soft music or recorded meditations helps amplify the bath's healing effects. Frequent showers also help to reinvigorate the senses and clear your personal energy.

Emotional Triggering and Heart Activation

Collective, ancestral, and individual trauma stored within the body's systems and DNA are being reactivated and cleared. Many experience this as a deep churning in the heart, fatigue, vivid dreams, and more. Aromatherapy is one of the quickest natural ways to soothe emotions.

Increased Intuitive Abilities

Intuition, psychic gifts, and multidimensional awareness are increasing rapidly as our lower energies clear out of the chakra and subtle energy systems, creating an expanded empathetic nervous system. To avoid unnecessary suffering and psychic attack, one can cultivate a strong and clear subtle energy system and grow in heart-centered discernment and energetic hygiene.

Vivid and Prophetic Dreams

Many are experiencing vivid dreams as their subconscious works out limiting beliefs and unprocessed trauma in their dreamtime. Some dreams are teaching dreams where people experience themselves in learning environments practicing new skills. Some are healing dreams where people report miraculous, rapid healing often conducted by extraterrestrial beings or higher light beings. Some people are reporting meetings with other souls in their soul group, where Ascension topics are discussed. Some people are reporting that they are being brought aboard spacecraft and introduced to galactic beings and receive updated intel on Earth changes and Ascension information.

Some people do not have any dream recall during the ascension process because the information being discussed in the dreams would keep them from playing out the role they need to in their regular human life. Some people have even traveled to the New Earth or future timelines where they get to experience life after humanity and Earth have ascended.

Each person is different in how they handle this process. Do not judge yourself based on how others are handling it. Also, one minute you can be fine, and the next minute have an emotional purge and a headache. Let the process happen. Make a practice of nourishing yourself.

This process can be intense, but it comes with great benefits! Thank you for facing your shadow and aligning with Truth, Knowledge, and Wisdom. You are so brave!

ELEVEN

Hand Placements: Self-Healing

There are various schools of thought that set hand placements for healing sessions. Some start from the crown and work towards the feet, and some do the opposite. Some methods use the chakra locations, and some include the major joints of the body. Every session is unique. All of the variety of hand placements are valid and useful. Here is a set that I use and teach to my students.

Intuitive Treatment for Self

1. *Gassho*: Ground, center, and tune into the Unified Field. Feel the subtle vibrations and amplify the sensations and connection with your breath. Feel your connection to Source and Gaia through your hara line. Evoke the emotions of Higher Love and Compassion. Feel your heart field expanding and strengthen your energetic field with Light and Love.

2. *Reiji-ho*: Connect with Universal Mind, divine guides, and your higher aspects. Welcome the infusion of your consciousness with the Wisdom and Presence of the Family of Light.

3. With hands in Reiji-ho, ask your Higher Awareness where you need healing.

4. Trust your internal messaging and allow your hands to be led to where they are needed.

5. Hover your hands above this target area, listen, feel, and trust what you receive through your Inner Being.

6. Transmit Love and Light from Source into the area you are treating. Invite wholeness and vitality and hold internal imagery of pure Light and Love. Use your breath to release excess energy that accumulates in your internal realm.

7. You may practice extraction or clearing practices or any other work you are guided to do here until the energy shifts to a balanced state. Often the hands will stop running energy as much when the target

area has taken as much energy as it needs. When you feel you have finished working with a target area, seal and bless the area with your intention.

8. Return to Reiji-ho and ask to be guided to the next area or immediately go to the next area if you are already receiving the following location in your awareness. Continue the process, keeping the mind focused on the intention of healing and compassion.

9. When finished, close with Reiji-ho to send gratitude for the assistance and connection to the higher realms. Use Gassho to ground, center, and strengthen your field. Be sure to bring your aura close to the body so that you feel contained and clear. Use Kenyo-ku to clear the body and finalize the transmission.

Scanning Method (Byosen Scanning)

In this method, I describe using your dominant and non-dominant hands for different steps. This is not a concrete rule. Try both and see which method works for you. It may even change over time. We are using the hands and senses to find distortions in the field.

1. Perform Gassho and Reiji-ho.

2. Hold your dominant hand off to the side and imagine, sense, and feel that it is holding a shiny ball of Source energy.

3. Using the non-dominant hand and starting with the palm facing the front of the Soul Star chakra, slowly bring the hand down the hara line, passing over each energy center.

4. Notice the sensations and listen to your internal messaging. Feel for any distortions or bumps in the field. Trust your intuition.

5. When you find distortion in the field, move the hand closer to the energy center and away until you feel the strongest, most noticeable layer of the distortion. Bring the other hands to meet side-by-side and channel fresh Source energy into the target area. Use your imagination to make it beautiful and radiant. Sweep and extract. Comb and fluff out the emanations of each center. Fill and seal with loving intentions.

6. When you feel the energy is balanced or the energy slows or stops

running from your hands, bring your dominant hand back up to hold the ball of Light and continue the hara line scan with your non-dominant hand, repeating the process wherever necessary.

7. Finish with Reiji-ho, Gassho, and Kenyo-ku.

Full Hand Placement Series

1. *Gassho*: Ground, center, call in, and activate the Light.
2. *Reiji-ho*: Connect with Universal Mind/Source, guides, higher aspects.

Soul Star Chakra

Bring the hands six to twelve inches above the head to connect with the Soul Star chakra. Trust your internal messages. You may feel the field of the Soul Star connect with the chakras in the palms of the hands as if "clicking" into place. Beam energy from your palms into the Soul Star while practicing deep, conscious breathing. Make it dazzle and sparkle with the brightest and clearest light. As you breathe in and out, imagine that fresh, Source Light is saturating the Soul Star chakra.

Crown Center

Bring the hands down to touch the crown of the head lightly. Move the hands closer and further away from the skin until you feel the edges of the Crown Center. Beam energy into the crown and use your imagination to clear, balance, and illuminate the Crown chakra. You may even want to use your fingers to comb and fluff the chakras to refresh them. Scrape and extract any energy that is stuck or stagnant, always filling and sealing with Light.

Brow Center and Face

Bring the palms down in front of the face, fingers pointing upward, and beam energy into the Brow chakra and upper face. Use your imagination to make the Brow chakra beautiful and radiant. Sweep and Extract. Comb and Fluff. Fill and Seal.

Zeal Center

Bring the hands to the back of the skull, fingers pointing up towards the crown, beaming Light into the occipital ridge/connection point between the spine and skull. This center is newly opening in many. You can use the thumbs to gently spread the energy open from the center of the chakra and outward to encourage the center to open. Sweep and Extract. Comb and Fluff. Fill and Seal.

Throat Center

Bring the hands to the side of the neck, close to the jawline and region of the thyroid gland, and beam Light into the Throat chakra. Use your imagination to make the Throat chakra beautiful and radiant. Sweep and Extract. Comb and Fluff. Fill and Seal.

Heart Center

Bring the right hand to lightly touch the High Heart chakra, right below the collarbone. Bring the left hand underneath of it at the Heart chakra center and beam Light into both of these centers. Use your imagination to make them beautiful and radiant. Sweep and Extract. Comb and Fluff. Fill and Seal.

Power Center

Face the palms towards the upper abdomen and lay them just below the diaphragm with the middle fingers touching and beam Light into the Power chakra. Breathe into your digestive organs. Use your imagination to make everything beautiful and radiant. Sweep and Extract. Comb and Fluff. Fill and Seal.

Back of Power Center (Optional)

Bring the palms to the back of the body and do the same process on the back of the upper rib area. Breathe into the back of the ribs as you beam Light into the Solar Plexus chakra. Use your imagination to make it beautiful and radiant. Sweep and Extract. Comb and Fluff. Fill and Seal.

Sacral Center

Front: Bring your palms to touch the lower abdomen or womb space lightly. Fingers may even make a triangle with the fingers meeting at the pubic bone, and the thumbs point towards or touching one another just below the naval. Beam Light into the Sacral chakra and organs. Use your imagination to make it beautiful and radiant. Sweep and Extract. Comb and Fluff. Fill and Seal.

Back: Bring your hands to the back of the pelvis/lower back, fingers meeting at the sacrum. Breathe into the organs and beam Light into the Sacral chakra. Use your imagination to make it beautiful and radiant. Sweep and Extract. Comb and Fluff. Fill and Seal.

Root Center

Option A: Bring the palms to the outside of the hips in alignment with where the femur head attaches to the hip socket (acetabulum) and beam energy to the Root chakra.

Option B: Bring the hands under the pelvis, cupping the hands over the perineum and beam Light into the Root Center.

Use your imagination to make it beautiful and radiant. Sweep and Extract. Comb and Fluff. Fill and Seal.

Feet and Earth Star Center

Bend your knee and adjust your posture in a way that you can cup one foot in your hand. Holding the hand approximately six to twelve inches away from the foot, beam Light from one of your hands to the entire foot, especially the sole of the foot. Use your imagination to make it beautiful and radiant. Soften your gaze and use your eyes to beam Light into the area you are working on. Sweep and Extract. Comb and Fluff. Fill and Seal. Repeat with the other foot. When finished, place both feet on the ground and tune into their magnetic connection to the Earth.

Beaming

If you cannot reach your feet, you can transmit the energy from your hands towards the area you are treating. Use your mind to visualize a powerful and healing stream of energy flowing from your hands to the area you are treating.

Full System Flush and Blossom

Bring the hands to rest on your knees or lap, perform Gassho or place your hands in prayer or any other position that helps you feel deeply connected with yourself. As you inhale, intend and imagine that you are breathing Light from Source down through your entire energy system, Soul Star to Earth Star. As you exhale, imagine that your whole system BLOSSOMS with Light. Continue breathing in and blossoming out until you feel radiant and bright.

After you have finished self-healing, this is a wonderful time to do distant healing or communicate with your higher aspects and guides. Your channel is now significantly brighter and open for higher communication. Use this time to visualize the highest potential outcomes for your day, week, or projects. When finished, seal your practice with Reiji-ho, Gassho, and Kenyo-ku:

Reiji-ho: Thank your higher aspects, guides, and Source. Dedicate your practice towards the benefit of all beings everywhere.

Gassho: Ground, center, and adjust the boundaries of your aura.

Use *Kenyo-ku* to clear off any stagnant energy and to stop the flow of Reiki consciously.

Additional Reiki Skills

Gyoshi-Ho: Transmitting Reiki with the Eyes

Eye contact plays a huge part in the transference of Light from one person to another object. As you look towards the object you wish to transform, soften your gaze, and consciously connect with Source, Gaia, and your breath. Imagine that loving, regenerative Source energy is shining from your eyes. Beam this Love from your eyes into everything that you see. Through your inner focus on Light, everything outside of you begins to transform into Heaven on Earth. There are unlimited ways to use this ability for self-healing and beyond. Everywhere you look, you can send healing energy!

If you find yourself around dense and/or chaotic energy, use your skills to ground, center, and broadcast Light into the field around you. Use conscious breathing to transmute the energy as it arises within and around you. Focus on Source as you anchor Light and watch as the dense or chaotic energies begin to shift. Use your inner sight to visualize the resolution, peace, and harmony, and broadcast this inner imaging into the field for others to source from. You will likely notice the circumstances in your outer experience shifting instantly as you anchor in a new potential into the timeline for everyone and everything to align with.

Koki-ho: Healing with the Breath

There may be times where you feel an area needs a strong dose of Light to clear and revitalize it. You can use the breath as a vehicle to transport healing energy and intentions for healing.

- Ground, center, and intend to connect with Source.
- On your inhale, breathe Source energy down through your hara line, filling your hara and entire being with Light from Source.
- You may also visualize a symbol or draw CKR or SHK on the roof of the mouth before you exhale. Exhale by contracting the abdomen strongly until you feel the pelvic floor contract. Direct the breath into the area that needs healing energy. Cover the area with your hands to seal in the healing energy with intention. You may also use CKR to seal the energy.

Clearing, Dedicating, and Charging Healing Objects

Many practitioners use various tools to support a healing session, including crystals, wands, singing bowls, pendulums, chimes, and so on. I believe it is important to clear the object of dense energies, dedicate it to the Light, and charge the object with Divine Energy before using it for healing or divination purposes.

- Ground, center, and establish a connection to the Light of Source.
- Hold the object or visualize the object in your mind.
- Using your dominant hand, chop above the object three times while synchronizing with sharp exhales as you intend to clear the object from dense or pervasive energies.
- Hold the object in your hands or in the light of your awareness and, using your intention or voice, dedicate the object to the Light for healing.
- Invite Source energy to flow through you powerfully into the object to charge it with light and healing vibrations. You may also visualize CKR, SHK, or any other healing symbol within the object's field.
- Intend that this energy will continue to renew and clear itself until you do it again.

Additional Energy Healing Skills

Drumming, Tapping, Padding

There may be times when you are called to drum lightly upon your body to direct vibrations into the muscles, connective tissues, and bones. Using the soft pads of your fingers and palms, lightly pat on the areas that are needing revitalization. Less is often more in the case of force. As you do this, use your imagination and breath to direct the vibrations into the dense parts and feel the energy breaking apart and disintegrating. After thirty seconds or so, stop drumming or tapping and cover the area with your palms, sealing the vibration and directing Light into the area. Use your breath to pull the healing energies deep into the target area.

Shaking

Shaking is a natural action performed by many species when they want to release energy. Imagine a dog shaking its whole body and the happiness they feel right after. You can use this technique to re-energize and clear stagnant energy.

1. Bring the feet under your pelvis or widen your stance a bit more. Stand tall and practice deep, conscious belly breathing.

2. Raise up onto the balls of your feet, lifting the heels. Begin to gently and rhythmically drop the heels to the ground and feel the vibrations traveling up your skeletal system. Feel the vibrations traveling through your muscles and tissues.

3. Imagine that old, stagnant energy simply falls away as the vibrations travel throughout the body. Use your breath and imagination to scan through the body and bring some extra shaking to those areas. Keep your face soft and allow the muscles of the face to shake as well. Especially shake the arms and hands to fling off any energies that are stuck there.

4. Imagine that Source is showering down clear, bright light that washes over you and recharges your system. Be playful, like a bird in a birdbath kissed by the Sun.

Toning/Sounding/Light Language

Using your ability to tone and sound is a powerful technology for clearing and activating energy. Different tones originate in different parts of the body. When linked with your mind and intention, you can direct the vibrations from the tones of your voice into various areas of your body and begin to heal.

1. Ground, center, and connect with Source, practicing deep and conscious breathing.
2. Take a long, deep inhale and begin to make a tone or humming sound. Play with it and find higher and lower tones that feel healing. Trust yourself and go for it, even if it feels silly at first. Generally, lower tones work with the lower chakras, and higher tones work with the higher chakras.
3. Using your hands and inner vision, lightly touch areas that need healing and begin to experiment with creating healing tones and direct them into the areas.
4. Play with different syllables using various consonant letter and vowel combinations and begin to create different combinations while holding the intention to heal and transmit Love and Light. Allow your heart to guide you as you transform the sounds into a Language of Light, harmonic tones that carry healing energies. Trust yourself and experiment with different sounds with a sense of joyful playfulness. Let your Inner Child come out to play!
5. When you have finished, bring your hands to a resting position, ground, center, and seal your field.

Cocooning with Light

When completing a session for yourself or someone else, you may choose to fill and seal the entire auric field. Intend that the cocoon will hold a healing container for the transformation to continue over the next few days and nights until the healing is complete.

Hold the hands wide out in front of you and imagine, sense, and feel that you are beaming bright, beautiful Source Light into your entire field. See it swirl and wrap around your entire being, filling and sealing up every part of you with healing, loving energy.

TWELVE

Facilitating Healing for Others

As you practice channeling Source energy, you become a healing presence for everyone and everything around you. People will begin to comment on how calm they feel around you and will likely begin to share deep parts of themselves with you because of the healing presence you emanate. Learning to facilitate a healing session for others is a skill that will come in handy as you and the world awaken to the Divinity that We Are. Energy medicine is the medicine of our ancient past and our future.

I suggest that people who desire to facilitate healing for others commit to self-healing for some time until they are comfortable with all the steps that I introduced in the previous sections for self-healing. Practicing self-healing gives you the experience of your own energy field to become aware of what is YOUR energy and what is not. It helps you trust your intuition and proficiency in the foundational skills for conducting a healing session. When you feel confident in your ability to connect with Source and channel Divine Energy for healing, you are ready to conduct a healing session for someone else.

Healing Presence

As you practice connecting with the Source and channeling divine energy, your energy field begins to transmute dense energies. It becomes saturated with high-frequency energy that raises the vibration of everything in your environment. This may look like people "lighting up" when you are around, and it may also trigger the lower energies and beliefs in some people. Many people learned to reduce their light because of trauma from the past, including childhood and even other lifetimes. I encourage everyone to push their edges more and more and learn how to stand tall and confident as they reclaim their sovereignty and embody the Light of their divinity.

Facilitating a Healing Session

Sharing reiki with others is natural and effortless as we learn to align with our True Nature. Conducting a healing session creates a deeply personal and heartfelt connection between the people who are involved.

When I was teaching energy healing under Usui Reiki's traditions, I found that people did not take a Level Two course because they did not want to be a practitioner who sees clients. While someone can certainly create a profession from energy healing sessions and counseling, I believe that facilitation is a skill for anyone to learn and share with those whom they love and want to support on their path of healing and awakening.

Imagine what a world we would live in where everyone had the foundational understandings of subtle energy medicine. Imagine what our cultures would be like if people practiced channeling Light from the Divine. Imagine what our world would look like if we all took responsibility to heal our own energy and support others through practices of healing and awakening. There would be no illness and disease. Our relationships would flourish. Every atom of life on the Earth would entrain to match the Light power of awakened humanity.

I will share the formal steps of conducting a healing session as if someone were seeing a client in a clinical setting. I will use the terms "practitioner" to refer to the one who facilitates the session and "client" for the one who receives the healing session. An informal session follows the same structure but may not necessarily contain all the same components because it is less formal. If you follow these simple steps and observances, you will know how to conduct a powerful healing session for a client or loved one.

While there are many benefits in learning how to facilitate a healing session for other people, including more skills, higher confidence, and the rejuvenating effects of facilitating a session, not everyone will find this information important for where they are NOW in their process. If this feels like you, please move forward to the next section of the book that speaks to you. You can always circle back when you are ready to explore further!

Divine Coordination of a Healing Rendezvous

I believe that these healing sessions are coordinated on higher planes before the session happens physically. This means that the Higher Self of the client and practitioner have agreed that meeting for a healing session would benefit both the practitioner and the client. Clients are drawn to a practitioner who has the skills they need to facilitate an appropriate healing session for that client. New practitioners can trust that whoever comes to them for healing is drawn to them because of what they can offer.

Clients may also be healing something similar to an aspect that needs to be healed in the practitioner. In this way, everyone benefits from the healing experience. Sometimes a client is brought to a practitioner because something about the healing session will teach the practitioner a new skill through higher guidance. Trust that whoever comes to you for healing is coming because you have everything needed to conduct an appropriate session for everyone involved.

All that is needed is a connection to our Inner Being and Source, intent to heal, and a willingness to listen to the energies and intuition.

Before a Client Arrives

Let us say that the appointment has been scheduled, and the client is about to arrive for the healing session. There are a few things you may want to do to prepare the session space and yourself.

Session Space

Once you learn how to do healing sessions for people, there is no limit to the conditions you will be invited to work with to create a healing space. I have performed sessions on kitchen tables, laying on the floor, in chairs, in hospital rooms, and more. Most practitioners, in the optimum conditions, use a massage table with blankets and sheets. Covering a client with a blanket connects them subconsciously with the feelings of getting ready for bed and will help them to relax right away. The blanket can always be adjusted or removed if the client gets too warm.

If you are using another surface, make sure there is some padding underneath the body as the client will be lying down for some time. Place something under the knees like a pillow or bolster to protect the lower back. You may even decide to use a chair if lying down is not comfortable for your client. Work with what you have.

Setting Up the Space for the Intake Interview

I set up two chairs for a pre-session conversation. Next to it, I may have tissues in case the client cries. I also have some paper and something to write with just in case either of us needs to make notes throughout the session. Sometimes I give clients "homework" or practices that they can do after the healing session, and it is important to write the steps down, so they do not forget.

When the client arrives, the lighting should be soft but on the higher side to see. Once we begin the healing session, I lower the lights to help create a relaxing atmosphere. Some people even like eye pillows to help them block out any extra light.

Music

Turn healing music on to bring healing vibrations into the room. Some "spa music" or "healing sounds" are too generic for me and may also be irritating for the client. I personally do not like flute music for some reason and tend to be drawn to more etheric tones like crystal bowls and soft chanting. Find out what your client likes and use those sounds to create a healing atmosphere. Be sure that you are using a system that will not have loud commercials interrupting the session's healing flow. Music will also help to drown out external noise like passing cars or other people. I have even used a "sound machine," a white/brown noise generator, to cancel outside noise. These can be purchased, or you can find pre-recorded white or brown noise recordings online.

Setting the Energy

Clear the room of stagnant or dense energy. You can do this in many ways. Smudge the space by burning aromatic plants, especially in the corners of the room. Open the windows to let the smoke out and fresh air in. Imagine that the walls are made of selenite crystals or that the walls are made of pure white healing energy. If the client is okay with essential oils, you may even diffuse something soothing, like lavender or a calming blend. Many people are extra sensitive to smells, so always ask your client what is appropriate before they arrive. What you may consider essential for a healing environment may not seem healing to another if they are sensitive or triggered. Visualize symbols or images in the space that promote well-being. Invite light beings to tend to the space so that the client feels the love energy right away.

Glass of Water

Get a glass of fresh water to set next to the treatment zone. The client may be thirsty when they arrive or need a drink during the session. I always have a client drink a glass of water after the healing session is complete to wash out toxins and re-lubricate the cells to support the ongoing healing process. You can charge the water with light beforehand to give it extra healing properties.

Hold the glass in your hand and imagine the molecules of water lighting up with golden-white light. Place intentions into the water molecules to support the healing process.

Gridding Up and Self-Treatment

Before the client arrives, connect with Source and ground the energies into Gaia. Begin running the energies and do a short self-treatment to ensure a healing presence when your client arrives. Whether you are aware of it or not, your client has started to tune into the session's healing energies from the moment the appointment was made. Use the time before the client arrives to tune into them psychically through intention and the power of nonlocal consciousness (remote viewing). You can send healing energy to them for their journey to the session. You may also receive intuitive, internal messaging about the client's needs before they arrive. Set the intention and visualize a successful session with lots of love being shared between you and your client. Use your voice to invoke divine healing energies, guides, and Source into the space. You may even want to stretch or do intuitive, flowing movement to lift your mood and open the body's energy channels since you will likely be standing for most of the healing session. Healing sessions should feel like a dance and doing some embodiment practice before the client arrives will help make the session more enjoyable for your body.

The Client Arrives

The moment the client walks into the room, be sure to welcome them and make eye contact warmly. Remember that your eyes, breath, and auric field are already beginning to work on the client's field. Have a feeling of love and welcoming in your energy. You do not have to be overly joyful; this may actually trigger someone who is in a state of agitation. A loving, clear presence is all that is needed.

Subliminal Messaging through the Voice

The tone of your voice should encourage relaxation and feelings of safety. Find ways to subtly suggest to your client that they will be having a deeply relaxing and rejuvenating healing session. Encourage them to let go and unwind and let them know this is a safe space to share whatever is in their heart. Broadcast inner imagery of well-being and joy into the space to connect with the client's Higher Self.

Opening the Field and Establishing Connection

I always start with a simple, short meditation to help both of us feel grounded, centered, and more deeply connected. I ask the client to feel into their heart and set an intention for the session. I want my client to feel a part of the healing process so that they do not rely on me solely for healing. My initial meditation always includes some form of breath awareness, hara line awareness, heart awareness, and an invocation of higher aspects and guides. This also establishes a psychic, empathetic link between myself and the client to receive internal messages and imagery that will help me support the client.

This meditation should be short, lasting between two to five minutes with guidance. Once it is complete, I ask the client what their intention is for the healing session. Then I ask if they have any physical health issues or areas of concern. I ask them what is happening in their life that needs balanced or healed. This conversation serves a few purposes.

- *Connection:* I want the person to trust me and trust the healing process.
- *Understanding:* I want to understand why they are here. I listen to the way they narrate their issues to understand what energy centers are misaligned and some potential focus areas for the laying of hands.
- *Guidance:* While listening to my clients, I often feel their blockages in my own body or receive internal messaging that will help the client and me somehow.

While listening, stay focused on your breathing, connected to your hara line, and gently nod your head at times to show that you understand and that you are listening. You can say "uh-huh," "that's natural," or other short phrases to let your client know that you hear them and that it is okay to be going through whatever they are going through. Many people carry so much shame because they feel that there is no safe space or that their emotions and beliefs are "bad." The intake interview is all about helping them accept themselves and be open to change while also letting them know that I am their unconditionally loving friend and guide.

Inspired Vision

Ask the client what their ideal situation is. Ask them what they want to create if they did not have any of the concerns that they currently have. This helps them start to manifest supportive energies and moves them out of victimhood/fate and into sovereign Divine Creatorship. You may even have them visualize this.

This can be as long or as short as needed for your client's needs and the time allotted. Most of the time, ten minutes covers the basics. Sometimes, clients want to share a bit more. I do not advise this during the interview phase. I simply want to hear what they want to share and help them relax.

Before starting, the client may need to use the restroom. It is a good idea to go anyway since they will be laying down for an hour or more. Once you feel they are comfortable and relaxed, you can begin the session.

The Session: Laying of Hands

Get your client into position for the healing session. Turn down the lights, turn up the healing music, and complete whatever other preparations you need to make. I like to sit for the first part of the session up above the head if my client is lying down. Much of the first part of the session is head-oriented, so having a chair placed above the head before beginning the session is helpful.

Once I have the client in position for the healing session, I take them through a process of breath awareness, unwinding, and intention setting.

Steps to Begin the Session

1. *Gassho:* Ground, center, and activate loving intention.
2. *Reiji-ho:* Welcome in guidance to support the healing session.
3. *Chiryo:* Begin the laying of hands.

There are various ways that a healing session can flow. Each session will be unique and beautiful. Allow yourself to be guided to where the energy is needed. Trust your internal messages. Some people like to stick to a certain set of hand placements. Others like to keep it free-form. I feel that a balance of both approaches is a sign of a proficient hands-on healer.

As I do the stages of grounding, centering, and opening to the healing energies in Gassho, I guide the client to do the same internal process. I guide them through the koshas, going through physical relaxation, life force awareness, relaxing the mind and intellect, and allowing them to rest in the Bliss Body. Progressive relaxation helps to release built-up tension in the physical body, tunes them into subtle energies, and slows down the brainwaves to create internal healing conditions. Doing some gentle breath awareness and breathwork calms the client's nervous system, connects them with their Inner Being, and opens their subtle bodies for healing.

Intention Setting

Intention setting rearranges the client's energy field for optimal healing and anchors the bodymind into coherence. I also tell my client softly that they can remain silent for the duration of the session and simply receive. I let them know that if they need anything, they can ask but that I will be mostly silent for the session. I let them know that they do not need to stay focused on me. They can even fall asleep if they would like! This is their opportunity to fully surrender and tune inward as they receive the soothing energies' benefits.

Invocation of Guides and Healing Energies

While I do Reiji-ho, I ask my client to invite the healing energies and the guidance of those who love and support them. I often say "Let us welcome your team of spiritual beings that lovingly guide and support your healing and evolution. Let us also welcome my team to support today so that we all work together towards harmony and vitality."

Laying of Hands

I like to start by sitting at the client's head and laying my hands on the client's shoulders. This helps them get used to light touch and establishes a connection between my body and theirs. Meanwhile, I lovingly beam Source energy from my eyes into the center of their heart while the energy begins to flow from my hands and entire being into their energetic field.

Practitioner Posture

It is important to keep your posture aligned and open during the session to allow proper flow. Breath awareness will help you keep soft length in the body and keep you focused on the present moment. If you find yourself drifting off with your thoughts, return to your breath, adjust and open your posture, and refocus on running energy for healing. Let the session feel like an intuitive dance. Playfulness helps to keep the spirit up.

Generally, the fingers of the hands should be closed and elongated to ensure the highest surface area is being covered. Thumbs should be connected to the side of the hand. Relax the shoulders and find a position where your body's bones are stacked comfortably. Never force yourself to stay in an uncomfortable position as this will affect the transmission of healing energy. Remember, your ENTIRE energy field is involved in the transmission.

Each hand position should be used for around five to ten minutes, depending on what is needed, and the time allotted for the session. New practitioners often feel like they need to move around or "do" a lot. I recommend "parking it" in a certain hand position for some time and simply running energy. It takes a few moments to feel the chakra open to receive the energy.

Method One: Standard Hand Placements

I do the first five hand placements sitting in a chair above the head of the client:

1. Hovering above the face.

2. Hovering to the side of the ears.
3. Under the occipital ridge (back of the head).
4. Hands on the crown with wrists in the center and fingers splaying out towards the ears.
5. One hand to the back of the neck and the other on the high heart. (Never place the hands on the front of the throat. This avoids triggering fear of choking.)

    For the next hand placements, I stand from my chair and walk clockwise around the body. You may choose to stand and do extra work on the heart. I often skip this as I already worked with the heart energies at the beginning of the session with my eyes and in hand placement #5 when I worked on the Throat Center.
6. Solar Plexus — upper abdomen above the navel.
7. Sacral Center — lower abdomen below the navel and above the pelvic bowl.

    For the Solar Plexus and Sacral centers, I place one hand behind the other so that one hand's fingers are touching the other hand's wrist as if I were measuring the width of their torso with my joined hands. Imagine that the torso is separated into four quadrants. The Solar Plexus is made of right and left sides, and the Sacral Center is made of a right and left side. Holding the hands this way ensures that you cover the whole "band" of that chakra's energy.
8. Root Center — Stand with your pelvis parallel to the table, one foot slightly in front of the other, and bring your hands to the outside of the client's pelvis. Use your imagination to visualize the Root chakra at the base of the tailbone.

    I typically skip the knees unless someone has knee problems. Some traditions have people work on the joints of the body. Play with it and see what feels right for you.
9. Feet — I often kneel at the client's feet and beam energy into their soles. You may also stand and hold the base of the feet by wrapping the fingers around the foot. Some people do one foot at a time, and some people do both at the same time. Find what feels comfortable for you.

Optional: Backside

Most of the time, I do not work on the back of the body because the front of the body easily takes an hour or more if I do five minutes or more at each hand position. There are many benefits from working on the back body, especially if the client has neck or back issues. So much gets stored in the spine and "roots" of the chakras that needs to be cleared away and revitalized.

1. Shoulders and Neck — Use the same stacked hand position that you used for the Sacral and Solar Plexus on the front of the body for all four chakra regions.
2. Back of Heart
3. Solar Plexus/Mid Back
4. Sacral Center/Lower Back

If a client begins to have an emotional release, do not interrupt them from their process. Continue holding an illuminated presence and allow them to feel their emotions. If it continues longer than a minute or two, ask them if they are okay and let them know you are here for them.

Method Two: Intuitive Hand Placement Session

Follow the same steps that you would use for a self-healing treatment. Use Reiji-ho to be guided to the places that are needing healing. Trust your guidance. Any time you get confused or are not certain what you need to do, return to Gassho and Reiji-ho to regain connection, clarity, and intuitive guidance.

Method Three: Scanning Method

Follow the same steps that you would use for a self-healing treatment. You may find that the area you are treating can be several feet above or outside of the body.

Method Four: Intuitive and Standard Hand Placements

Begin with the Scanning Method to find the most obvious distortions in the field. Next, you can follow the standard hand placements or do intuitive hand placements. Finish with the Scanning Method to see what else is needed.

Wrapping It Up: Cocooning with Light

Stand a few feet away from the recipient so that you can see their entire body. Stand tall in your connection to Source, face the palms towards the recipient and beam pure, loving Source energy into their entire field. Wrap them in blessings. Imagine them joyfully celebrating their new path. Send gratitude to Source and the guides that assisted in the healing session. You can use symbols to seal and amplify the intentions of the healing session. (*See Channeling Hands Mudra.*)

Finishing the Session

Often clients fall asleep during the healing session or, at the least, have entered a trance state. Take time to bring them back into conscious awareness slowly. The first time you speak should be gentle like you are waking the most adorable infant from sleeping. The client should be able to feel the joy and love in your voice as you awaken them.

Bringing Them Up

Speaking gently and softly, you can guide your client back to full consciousness saying something similar to the following:
1. Begin to gently come back into your body, deepening and elongating the breath. As you breathe, imagine that you are breathing in all the healing energies from the session.
2. Set an intention for your path. Maybe it is to live peacefully or to be loving. Allow your intention to come from your own heart.
3. Begin to gently move your fingers and toes as you take control of the body and begin to wake up now.
4. Begin to hear the sounds around you and the sounds of your body as it moves and you awaken. Become aware of the space and my presence next to you as you wake up now.
5. Almost fully awake now, yawn or stretch as you fully take control of your body.

6. Open your eyes slowly and be here now, feeling refreshed and revitalized.

I like to give the client a few minutes to continue the waking-up process on their own. I tell them that I will leave the room for a few minutes, and they can slowly continue to wake up. I let them know that a glass of water is next to them, and I would like for them to drink it to flush the body. I let them know that I will knock on the door before I re-enter the space.

Once I leave the room, I use the time to do Kenyo-ku, wash my hands, splash cold water on my face, or even shake my bones to get me grounded and centered.

Post-Session Conversation

I spend a few minutes talking with the client about their session to ensure that they are grounded enough to drive. I ask them to tell me about their experience, and I share any insight that may have come to me during the session. Use discernment when relaying intuitive messages and guidance. This is the perfect time to recommend practices to support continued healing.

If you receive inner messaging about serious health issues, please direct them to get proper medical advice from a skilled physician. Be careful to do this in a way that does not generate fear. Disclose that what you received may or may not be true for them, but you are relaying messages you received. Now that we have closed the session, this is the time where I take payment for the session and offer to make a follow-up appointment.

Once They Leave

Use this time for personal and distant healing since you are probably quite charged after the session. Break down the space and clear the energies using smudging herbs or other techniques.

You can also dedicate a self-healing session to another recipient. I love this because both of you get the benefits of the healing session!

Distant & Remote Healing (Enkaku Chiryo)

There will likely be times when you will want to share energy healing with someone you cannot be with physically. We are all connected within the Unified Field of Creation, and distant healing is a powerful tool for us to feel connected with people and places outside of our physical environment through nonlocal consciousness.

Pillars of Distance/Remote Healing

Successful distant healing comes down to three points: **Compassion**, **Intention**, and **Attention**.

Holding the recipient in your awareness (*attention*) with the *intention* to transmit healing energy links your consciousness to the person, place, or object that you are desiring to support. While meditating on the transmission, continuously renewing a sense of unconditional love amplifies the potency of the transmission.

The Reiki symbols help establish a link by training you to focus on a healing intention but are not necessary for creating a successful and powerful healing transmission across space and time. This ability is given to you through your connection to Source, and the symbols help train you to fine-tune that ability. Many find value in using the symbols at first, then gradually release the tool once they are used to connecting.

Use Gassho and Reiji-ho to prepare the energy for the transmission. Say a declaration to state who you are sending the energy to and where they are in the world. You can also simply pull an image of them into your mind. Keeping an internal image of them or repeating their name mentally or out loud helps strengthen the link and amplify the intentions.

Methods of Remote Healing

Surrogate Method

You can also dedicate a self-healing session to another recipient. I love this because both of you get the benefits of the healing session! When in Reiji-ho, set the intention for the healing to go to whomever or wherever you wish to send healing.

Leg Method

The leg method is effective because you can do a full body session in a short amount of time. This is the method I use the most since my legs and hands are always with me. Find a seated position and dedicate the healing session to a certain person by stating or thinking their name or by bringing an image of that person into your mind. You may also choose to use the Distant Healing Symbol from the Usui System.

Dedicate one thigh of your body to be the front of that person's body, and the other thigh will symbolize the back of that person's body. Starting at the kneecap, symbolizing that person's head, begin to run energy into your thighs, imagining that the person is receiving the energy into their body. After some time, move the hands further up your thighs until you reach your pelvis. You may receive intuitive guidance during the session. Please follow the guidance just like you would for a healing session.

Picture Method

Take a picture of the person, place, or situation you want to send healing to. Hold the photo in your hands or prop the photograph up and beam energy into the picture. Use positive internal imagery and conscious breathing to amplify the intention.

Teddy Bear Method

This is a simple practice where you use a stuffed animal as a stand-in for a healing session. The best stuffed animal to use will have two arms, a head, a torso, and two legs like a human. As you do Gassho, say out loud or state internally that you are dedicating this session to whoever is intended to be the recipient. Continue with the session as you normally would with a client. It will likely be much shorter since your hands cover much of the body.

Starting an Energy Healing Business

For many, starting a business as a healer seems like a natural step in their lives, and for others, it may seem way beyond their edge or comfort zone. I think it is important that there be reciprocation when conducting healing sessions for others. Many healers feel as if they give, give, give, and never have enough energy for themselves and no money to pay the bills. A lot of time and energy goes into developing a healing business beyond the actual healing session. If you are like me, you are working non-stop. I suggest starting with a lower price or a suggested donation price and slowly working your way up until you find the amount that feels good for you to receive and that the clientele you like to work with can afford.

Those who offer healing services often invest a lot of money, time, and energy in fine-tuning their craft and marketing it to the world. This is part of the reason why healers charge for their services. While there is nothing "bad" about charging for healing sessions, we should also make our services accessible to people who need healing and guidance. This can be done in several ways, including bartering, trades, a certain number of donation-based sessions per month, and so forth. Remember, while we do need to earn an income, we can find ways to share our services in a way that is sustainable and accessible to those who need it most.

Attracting People to Share Reiki With (Clients)

There are many ways to manifest or attract others who would be appropriate to work with. I suggest being clear with what you intend to manifest. What type of people do you like to work with? Are they paying or non-paying clients? Do you travel to them, or do they come to you? All these details are important to add to the specifics of what you are calling into your path as a healer.

Meditation for Attracting People for Healing Sessions

1. Take some time to ground, center, and connect with the Light of Source.
2. Visualize the types of beings you want to work with.
3. Imagine that a golden thread is reaching from your heart center and connecting with all those beings to let them know you are available to support them.
4. Imagine how happy they will be to know that someone wants to

help them along their path. Visualize them coming for successful sessions and happily paying or blessing you in some other way because of the benefit of the session.

5. Continue to play with this for a few minutes. Send gratitude out to all the supporting energies for this work.

Group Healing: Many Hands Make Light Work

I highly encourage organizing small or large group gatherings where people share and receive Source-sent healing energies. Someone can guide the group to help everyone synchronize intentions and connect with Source for energy healing. Healing sessions are shorter when done in a group because there are extra hands to cover more areas of the body.

1. Everyone gathers around the person who is going to receive energy healing. Stand a few feet away and begin with Gassho to help them connect with them and to feel the energy of the group.

2. Bring the hands to Reiji-ho to invite higher aspects and guides into the space.

3. Slowly approach the recipient and begin to lay hands wherever you are called to. Feel the power of light moving from the higher realms, through your bodies, and into the recipient. Feel many beings supporting the process and broadcasting their loving vibrations into the group field.

4. When the segment with that client is finished, cocoon the client with light as a group.

5. Use Kenyo-ku to clear and disconnect the energy and prepare for the next client by repeating Gassho and Reiji-ho.

Meditation Script

This meditation script can be read to another person to guide them into meditation, or you can record it yourself to make a guided meditation for your own practice.

Go ahead and move into a comfortable position for seated meditation where you can easily sit with a long spine. You can use pillows, blankets, or any other props to make yourself more comfortable. You can sit in a chair, against the wall, or simply sit up with a long spine. If seated meditation is uncomfortable for you, you can do the practice laying on your back. Soften your gaze or close your eyes and begin to tune inward to the more subtle parts of your experience.

(*Slight pause and allow people to settle in.*)

Notice the physical body and its sensations. Scan through the body to see if you can adjust your posture so that you can sit tall and comfortably. Allow the weight of the pelvis to drop into the ground, stacking each vertebra as you rise up the spine. Gently draw the shoulder blades together to open the chest, allowing the shoulders to open wide as if you were proudly wearing a beautiful necklace. Lengthen the back of the neck by gently drawing the chin toward the chest so that the crown shines towards the sky or ceiling.

(*Pause*)

Notice your breathing patterns and the movement of life force in and around your body. Begin to deepen and elongate the breath. Take long deep inhales to open the body and long, deep exhales to release any unnecessary tension or holding patterns. Use your breath to sweep through and restore all of the energy of your body. Allow yourself to be deeply nourished and revitalized by the breath.

(*Pause*)

As you breathe consciously, notice the mind and the thoughts. Allow the thoughts to drift by like clouds in the sky as you bring your awareness back to the breath and back to the present moment. At any time that thoughts arise, allow them to exist and drift away gently as you bring your awareness back to the breath.

(*Pause*)

Notice the part of you that is observing these experiences, the part of you that witnesses the body, the energy, and the breath. Notice the part that recognizes that "I am meditating." Feel your wisdom body, your ability to understand, and your ability to receive flashes of insight and guidance. If any stories or thoughts arise, allow them to dissolve as you rest in the witnessing part of your consciousness.

(*Pause*)

Expand your awareness and feel your connection to the Universe. Feel yourself expanding in this connection with all of Life. Intend to connect with your inner joy, inner peace, and your willingness to serve the goodness of Life.

(*Pause*)

Imagine that far above your head is a bright star shining with golden-white light. This radiant star symbolizes the Source of All Life, the loving presence of God. As you inhale, invite this pure light to flow down through your central channel, passing through the crown of your head and filling your entire pelvic bowl. As you exhale, send the energy downward anchoring yourself deep into Gaia, Mother Earth. As you breathe in and out, allow light to sweep away any stagnant, unneeded energy and release it into the Earth for composting. Each breath fills you with fresh light. Each exhale anchors you deeply into the Earth.

(*Pause*)

Feel into the core of Gaia. Feel into the loving, evolutionary pulsations of the energy of Mother Earth. As you breathe in, breathe her loving energy up into your own heart center, and as you exhale, send the energy back to Source, back to the star above your head. As you breathe, in and out, bridge the heart of Gaia, your own heart, and the heart of Creation, centering yourself in this Divine Love.

(*Pause*)

Breathing energy from above and from below, from Gaia and from Source, fill your central channel with Love and Light. As you exhale, send that energy in all directions around you, filling your entire auric field with Light and Love. Make your field strong and clear. Notice where your energy ends and where the rest of the world begins. Make your space feel sacred and beautiful.

(*Pause*)

Bring your awareness to your own heart center, to the core of your being, and set an intention for your meditation, a simple intention from the heart. Maybe it is Peace. Maybe it is Love. Maybe it is Presence. Set your intention and allow yourself to settle into your heart, into the spaciousness of love and presence, simple being. If any thoughts arise, notice them and allow them to pass by as you rest in loving awareness. We will be quiet for some time, and I will bring you back after _____ minutes.

(*Meditation*)

The facilitator should be meditating as well as holding space. Set a timer if needed. You can also be sending Light to all who will join the meditation. Clear any dense energy that may arise within you, intending that this also be cleared for the other meditators.

Bringing Them Back

One suggestion to facilitate the gentle return of the meditators is to read them something inspiring such as a quote, a poem, or part of a sacred text. This starts to bring them out of *anandamaya kosha* and back into *vijnanamaya kosha*, the observing part of the consciousness.

You can then address them with loving instructions: Alright, start to come back now bringing all of this awareness, Light, and Love with you.

Keeping the eyes closed, begin to deepen the breath as you become aware of the space you are in. Take deep full breaths as you begin to take control of the body again with a feeling of plenty of time. Begin to slowly stretch the body, enjoying the pleasure of movement as you breathe life into the body.

Let us meet with eyes closed and hands in prayer position at the heart.

Bow the mind to the heart, honoring the wisdom and guidance of the heart. Set an intention for your path. Let it be simple and let it be of love.

(*Pause*)

Bring the prayer hands up to the Brow Center, touching the thumbs against the forehead. Dedicate the fruits of this practice to something beyond yourself. Maybe it is for the liberation of all beings from cycles of suffering. Maybe it is for your family or a loved one. Maybe it is for Mother Earth. Send this love out to all who can benefit from it.

Bring the hands to rest on the lap or bow forward in reverence and gratitude. When you are ready, bring yourself to seated, slowly open your eyes, and allow the Light to come to you as it always has and always will.

Group Prayer and Light Anchoring

There are many ways that a community can come together in prayer to anchor in Light and Love for communal and global healing. For me, the most powerful group prayers honor the Higher Realms, Gaia, the Inner Earth families, and our family from the stars.

1. Sit together in a circle and face inward towards the center of the circle and discuss the focus of prayer for the group. This may be a unified vision or a collection of individual issues. If it is a person that is present and they are comfortable with the attention, you may even place them in the center of the circle to receive.

2. Each member of the circle then connects with their own pillar of Light and sacred heart. This bridges the realms of Light with the Earth. Broadcast a beam of love from the heart towards the center where it is united and merged with the projections from the other group members to create a bright, dazzling star of golden-white light.

3. Welcome guides and spiritual allies to join in the prayer. As the group holds the prayer field in unified intention, visualize the highest potential timelines for resolving what is needed to bring the situation to balance.

4. Amplify the prayer field by singing, toning, or activating Light language together. You may even choose to hold hands and circulate the energy to the left to create a powerful vortex within the prayer field. When holding hands in a circle, I always cue for everyone to turn their thumbs to the left to create balance within the circle.

5. Allow this to continue until the energy subsides.

6. Ground, center, and solidify your own personal auric field once the prayer is complete.

7. Stay in a circle and talk as a community about what insights or experiences may have occurred during the prayer. Share your deepest truths with one another. Join in one heart and witness one another with loving kindness and eternal friendship.

ASCENSION LEXICON

I have put together a list of words commonly used in this book and for the topics of awakening, spirituality, and ascension. These are not necessarily defined this way by others but are an excellent way to understand my writings in this book in a more clear and multidimensional way.

-A-

Adamic Form: Original perfected divine human form created for highly developed Light Beings to experience physical creation from within the physical dimension. Fourth Density (4D) body of the New Earth human connecting with oversoul consciousness, higher dimensional beings, and telepathic species.

Agartha: Ancient Inner Earth multi-species civilization with its own sun and ecosystem within the Earth. See *Inner Earth.*

Ain Soph: Kabbalistic term for Source before manifestation into form and translates to "Without Limit" as it is the unlimited creative potential behind all of Creation. Same as "Ineffable" in the Gnostic texts. Can also be written as "Ensof."

Akashic records: Higher-dimensional spiritual records of all experience past, present, and future. Each soul has one. So does each planet and so on.

alchemy: The application of spiritual knowledge to matter to create transformation. This is more commonly known with the Middle Ages' pursuits of turning simple metals into gold. High alchemy being the alchemy of soul/lightbody.

Ancient Egypt: Last golden age of Gaia when many beings held 4th, 5th, and 6th-dimensional consciousness before the descent into lower consciousness (forgetting).

Andromedans: Highly advanced star beings from the Andromeda galaxy assisting humanity's ascension.

Anunnaki: Star beings from the Nibiru system. Sumerian space "gods" who manipulated humanity for personal gain. Now most are in support of humanity's ascension.

apocalypse: 1. Greek word for "unveiling." 2. The dismantling of the mind control matrix and false projections from the controlling forces to reveal to humanity the ugly underbelly and karma of the collective consciousness upon the Earth from this creation cycle which is to be fully reconciled before the planet changes in dimension to Fourth Density New Earth. Not the "end" but a transitionary phase into the next creation cycle.

Archons/Controllers: Term used to describe negatively polarized service-to-self, nonphysical, intelligent beings who siphon negative energy from humanity for their own gain using mind control tactics to keep humanity enslaved through fear and distorted consciousness. The controlling forces behind global institutions. Will be fully dismantled before the shift to New Earth.

Arcturians: Star beings from the constellation of Arcturus assisting Earth with Ascension.

Ascension/ascension: 1. The spiritual maturity process of a soul, moving from an unawakened state of mundane consciousness to multidimensional Source/God-realization described as the movement of the kundalini up the central channel, samadhi, moksha, nirvana, salvation... 2. The movement of Creation into greater states of Glory. 3. The current collective planetary transformation from 3D to 5D consciousness and the New Earth reality.

ascension symptoms: Physical, etheric, mental, and spiritual changes during ascension cycles. Includes headaches, emotional purging, detoxifications symptoms, multidimensional DNA reprogramming, body aches, vivid dreams, and beyond.

Ascended Master: Level of spiritual hierarchy of beings who have ascended in their consciousness enough to no longer need to incarnate in form for spiritual growth but may choose to incarnate to assist the ascension process of a species.

Atman: Divine origin identity, True Self, True Nature, the Witness Consciousness of a lifestream. Same as Brahman. Source Self. Eternally free.

aura: Electromagnetic field of subtle energy that surrounds and pervades the physical body. Contains ever-shifting patterns and geometries of light and vibration that create the template for the physical form.

-B-

biotransducer: organic instrument for transforming energy information for the purpose of manifestation and communication with the universal hologram and divine frequencies. Able to utilize advanced intelligence and spiritual information for the transformation of reality in the human environment.

bodhisattva: Sanskrit term for someone on the path of Buddhahood (ascension) who dedicates their path to the liberation of all beings from cycles of suffering. Able to achieve liberation but delays to assist others in consciousness expansion.

Brahman: The Absolute Reality. Source in impersonal, nonmanifest state. Pure Infinity Existence Consciousness Bliss, *Satchitananda*.

buddhi: the Intellect, reflected consciousness, enlightened consciousness in each person.

buddhic consciousness: enlightened consciousness expressed by *buddhi*, the vehicle for the soul, experienced as profound intuitive insight, unity, and bliss.

-C-

Cabal: Global elite network of negatively polarized service-to-self operatives and organizations working towards complete domination of humanity and planet Earth. See *Archons.*

causal consciousness: the higher mind capacity which utilizes soul memory and intuition to observe and understand manifestation multidimensionally.

centering: Alignment with one's divine nature and inner truth, activating a bridge between Gaia and the Divine through the heart center.

centropy: Regenerative electrification of matter-energy.

chakras: Spiraling transformers of subtle energy with seven primary vortices emanating from the central channel (*sushumna*) which govern our perception of the projected holographic reality and energize our mental and physical processes.

channeling: Opening one's consciousness and vessel as a conduit for subtle energy or other consciousnesses.

Christ: 1. Yeshua ben Joseph (Jesus) in his ascended Lightbody. Forerunner of christ consciousness as part of a divine plan for redemption and restoration of humanity and Earth back to a 4th Density collective. 3. A collective consciousness field that has many emanations and incarnated forms throughout the history of Creation. 4. Title given to one who has achieved consciousness mastery and is "anointed" by Light.

christ consciousness: Also called cosmic consciousness or 5D consciousness. Demonstrated by Jesus of Nazareth in his resurrected 4th Density body.

Christ/Magdalene Lineage: Genetic implantation of higher DNA coding through the offspring of Jesus and Mary. Descendants are worldwide and able to carry a higher light quotient and awaken more easily.

clairaudience: Clear hearing is the ability to hear messages from your Higher Self or spirit beings. This includes hearing the thoughts of other people.

clairgustance: Clear tasting is the ability to receive intuitive information through the sense of taste.

clairesalience: Clear smelling is the ability to intuit information through the sense of smell.

clairvoyance: Clear sight is the ability to perceive information through internal imagery.

clear channeling: Mediumship, or spirit channeling, is the ability to communicate with nonphysical beings and consciousness structures. This can include souls who have passed beyond the veil of physical life or beings that exist in other dimensions.

collective: Representing an entire group, i.e., human collective.

Collective Messiahship: The unification of ascending humanity with the intention of global restoration and ascendency.

cords: Subtle energy attachments that connect us to other beings. Can be negative if developed through limiting beliefs and distorted conditioning.

council: Group of beings joined together with a common focus (i.e., your spiritual council of guides who support your spiritual maturation across lifetimes).

Councils of Light: Groups of advanced spiritual beings that govern the evolution of consciousness and the biological forms of a certain experimental zone to encourage higher states of glory and harmony with the highest being the Universal Council of Light.

-D-

density: 1. Mass per volume. 2. Bandwidth of consciousness reality.

Descension/descension: To go down. The forgetting or falling asleep phases of consciousness. The stepping down of light frequency.

dharma: The noble path of awakening guided through alignment with the Divine through one's True Nature. Exemplified by the life path of beings like Jesus and the Buddha.

The Divine: The frequency emanation that governs and sustains all of Creation across many universes within universes. God Source and the Hosts of Heaven. See *Godhead*.

Divine Androgyny: Harmonic synergy between the divine masculine and divine feminine energetic expressions that results in perfect balance and cohesion.

Divine Creatorship: The birthright of a human to create their life with free-will choice in alignment with their Inner Source.

Divine Feminine: 1. Nurturing creative quality of the Divine 2. Archetypal, spiritual, and psychological ideal of the feminine energetic expression.

Divine Masculine: 1. Administrative quality of the Divine 2. Archetypal, spiritual, and psychological ideal of the masculine energetic expression.

DNA: Genetic blueprint for the development of an organism with both physical and subtle components. Ascended humanity will have 12 fully restored strands.

-E-

Earth Changes: Physical and subtle energetic changes that occur on the planet as it prepares to shift into the next creation cycle. Includes pole shifts, weather changes, seismic and volcanic activity, electromagnetic shifts, and more.

Elohim: First Creation. Creator beings with individual consciousness that work in groups to form Creation. Some created as service-to-all working in unity with Source. Some were created as service-to-self permitted to create in the illusion that they were separate from Source.

empath: Individual who is sensitive to the subtle energy such as thought, and emotional projections of others as they intuitively feel the mental/emotional body of others within their own mental/emotional realm. See *clairsentience*.

End Times: The closing of this current creation cycle where all karma must be balanced, and all shadow revealed so that Earth and spiritually activated humanity can begin the next creation cycle in 4th Density New Earth. See *apocalypse*.

energy: Subtle energy beyond the visible light spectrum ranging from pervasive to neutral to regenerative and life-enhancing. Everything is energy.

energy awareness: Perception of subtle energy in and around one's body.

energy matrix: Geometric organization of subtle frequencies that creates the base structure for the development of form.

entity attachment: Astral debris that has attached itself to a weakened energy system of a host as a source of sustenance and a way to live out "unfinished business." Quite common and easily resolved most of the time by a trained spirit releasement practitioner or energy medicine practitioner.

entropy: Decay and degeneration of matter-energy.

extraterrestrial: From outside of the Earth's biosphere including other planets and universes. There are countless species in our solar system, galaxy, super galaxy, and beyond. Infinite species in infinite realms of creation with many advanced civilizations with histories tracing back trillions of years.

evolution: See *Higher Evolution.*

-F-

false prophets: Teachers and prophets who use spiritual information for service-to-self agendas. Many religious leaders, spiritual teachers, and even those in the ascension community will have their true intentions revealed in the final phases of Ascension.

Family of Light: Physical and nonphysical beings who live their lives in alignment with the Oneness of Creation and the Divine Source. Includes the races of the Star Nations who hold 5D consciousness and higher and the Hierarchy of Light who tend to the many levels of Light Creation.

5D: Consciousness of humans living on the New Earth, can be referred to as christ consciousness or oversoul consciousness.

4D: Awakening stage of ascension bridging mundane consciousness with the New Earth consciousness.

frequency: 1. Rate of vibration measured in hertz (Hz). 2. Higher vibrational rate is likened to positivity and centropy and lower rate towards negativity and entropy.

-G-

Gaia: 1. Sentient Earth 2. Common name for the soul of Earth. Also called Terra.

Galactic Federation of Light: Intergalactic and ultraterrestrial collective of advanced beings who tend to the evolution of consciousness and biological forms throughout the Milky Way. Comprised of advanced scientists, engineers, medical personnel, and other areas of expertise needed to maintain order and balance in the galaxy.

genetic implantation: Seeding of new DNA into the gene pool to evolve a species into higher states of harmony or functionality. Used by the Star Nations and Hierarchy of Light to craft zones of biological experimentation.

gnosis: Direct experience of divine nature through one's own inner being and inner knowing that leads to higher understanding of the nature of the divine reality. See *Knowledge*.

Great Central Sun: Source of all levels of creation in this universe. Brings higher evolutionary coding from Divine Source into other central suns in the universal grid which flow to each solar system evolving each region in accordance with a Divine Plan for Higher Evolution. See *Ishawara*.

Great Divide: The bifurcation of consciousness amongst humanity during the end phases of the planetary ascension process. Includes physical movement across the Earth as humanity moves to be with others of shared consciousness and similar vibration and soul path. Two-world-spit of those who hold negatively polarized, service-to-self consciousness and those of positively polarized, service-to-all consciousness.

Great White Brotherhood: More accurately **Great White Siblinghood**. Ascended Masters, human and non-human, of all gender expressions organized into different orders or councils who tend to the evolution of consciousness and sometimes incarnate to bring new teachings and new energy. Many of these Ascended Masters have aspects of themselves on the planet now to assist the Ascension.

Greys: Extraterrestrial beings from Zeta Reticuli.

God: 1. Supreme Source of Creation 2. Divine Masculine, administrative quality of Godhead, Eternal Mind. See *Ishwara*.

Goddess: 1. Divine Feminine, nurturing, regenerative, creative aspect of the Godhead. 3. Mother God.

Godhead: The Divine Consciousness Source and its various emanations and functions.

Golden Ages: Times of high consciousness and harmony upon the Earth during the Precession of the Equinoxes. (e.g., Avalon, Lemuria)

grounding: The anchoring of one's physical and subtle bodies into the Earth's core through intention, diaphragmatic breathing, and visualization through the Root and Earth Star chakras.

guides: Spiritual beings who assist an incarnated being on their dharmic path towards liberation.

-H-

hara line: Central pillar of light connecting an individual with Gaia and Source.

heart-centered: Action born from inner truth and spiritual ethics through alignment with one's divine nature.

Hierarchy of Light: Various levels of divine consciousness forms, aspects of Source that serve different functions in the evolution of Creation. Ain Soph/Source, Elohim, Archangels, Angelic Realm, Ascended Masters, Ascended Goddesses, Interdimensional Beings, and Restored Humanity in Adamic Form. The Hosts of Heaven.

Higher Evolution: Beyond biological evolution and natural selection, the recoding of experimental zones of the hologram of Creation using divinely encoded frequencies projected through the stellar network which are coordinated by benevolent beings, physical and nonphysical, who serve the evolution of the Divine Plan throughout the Multiverse. Also includes introduction of new genetic expressions into the gene pool, new technologies, and new ideas to be used to evolve the creation into higher order.

Higher Self: 1. The mature part of our consciousness which operates in positively polarized, service-to-all consciousness and is connected to our divine nature. 2. Sovereign self. 3. Harmonic Divine/Human synthesis. 4. Oversoul. 5. Atman.

Holding space: A term used in spiritual growth and self-development circles that means "to hold suffering in an alchemical container of loving awareness so that it may heal."

Holy Spirit Shekinah: The feminine regenerative energy of the Divine. The "presence of God" in the physical dimension. Opening yourself to channel the divine presence begins an alchemical process of light activation that heals and restores all levels of one's being.

-I-

Inner Earth: Ancient and contemporary subterranean civilizations. Many beings went to Inner Earth before the destruction of Lemuria and

Atlantis. See *Agartha*.

intention: Inner resolve to direct one's focus and creative capacity towards a specific goal. *Sankalpa* in Sanskrit.

interdimensional: Existing between dimensions.

intuition: The ability to perceive energy information beyond the five senses before it has become physically manifested in reality. 2. Extrasensory perception.

involution: spiritual consciousness activation that begins as one moves through Ascension and sheds the mind's conditioning.

Ishwara: 1. personal expression of Source. 2. Source in purest manifested form. Commonly called "God" 3. Great Central Sun. 4. Universal Logos.

-J-

Jesus/Yeshua ben Joseph: Master of Light for Earth. Twin flame of Mary Magdalene. Supreme teacher of Divine Love and Ascension. Brought restored DNA and pure Christ Light to the Earth to activate the 4th Density Redemption Plan. Yeshua's cosmic oversoul legacy includes many star systems including the high spiritual schools of Light in the Pleiades and Sirius A and B. His arrival into this dimension of space was the Star of Bethlehem Lightship. His life path was supported by many galactic beings incarnated upon the Earth as well as many extraterrestrials and ultraterrestrial beings. 2. Incarnation of Ascended Master Lord Sananda.

-K-

karma: 1. The sum of a being's actions in this life and in previous existences, both positive and negative actions which influences the soul's path through incarnations.

Knowledge: "Gnosis," divine insight that activates higher consciousness and God-realization. Sanskrit *aparoksha*

kundalini: Serpentine energy originating at the base of the spine that ascends through the sushumna during the awakening process creating ecstatic spiritual expression.

-L-

Lemuria: First advanced human civilization. Often associated with the Pacific Ocean. Destroyed by major flooding and earth changes.

ley lines: Subtle energy pathways that carry evolutionary information across the planetary grid. Also called dragon lines, songlines, telluric lines.

Light: Regenerative divine energy emanations that exist beyond the typical visible light spectrum (Holy Spirit). Different than conventional light from lightbulbs.

Light beings: 1. General term for nonphysical beings of divine origin. See *Family of Light.*

lightbody: 1. subtle body 2. Vital, lower, and higher mind sheaths. 3. Transmigrating soul

Light Conception: The act of conceiving a child directly from the spiritual realms without the need of sperm from a physical being.

Light language: 1. Language spoken through connection to the Divine Presence. Activates multidimensional healing and powerful internal experiences with healing frequencies. Gift of the Holy Spirit, the regenerative creative frequency that quickens and restores all levels of Life. Can be self-initiated or pushed through from the Higher Self and the Divine.

Light Seed: Higher-dimensional, light-encoded genetic material used for Light Conception and altering the genetic composition of a species. Aka *Immaculate Conception.*

Lightship/lightship: Divine craft made by one individual's lightbody/merkaba or a merged merkaba from more than one being for the purpose of interdimensional travel through space-time, stargates, and higher light realms.

Love: Beyond egoic love, unconditional love that is naturally expressed when one develops love for the divine and a service-to-all intention. *Agape* love.

lokas: Sanskrit word for the planes of existence.

loosh: energy of suffering and death harvested by negative human, extraterrestrial, and interdimensional beings which is used to fuel nefarious agendas.

Lyrans: Star beings from the constellation of Lyra. Most commonly known race is the feline beings. First humanoid race in the Milky Way. Original 144,000 oversoul starseeds to bring the human species to Earth.

-M-

magic(k): Use of universal, natural law, and intention to manifest. Can be either service-to-self (dark) or service-to-all (light).

manifestation: The materialization of intention into form.

mantra: Holy names and phrases repeatedly spoken or thought which generate divine thoughtforms to reprogram the physical, etheric, and mental bodies opening one's consciousness to higher perception, divine insight, and union with the Divine. Use of mantra repatterns the DNA, clearing distortion and debris and reprogramming it into higher order and functionality for the projection of divine consciousness light.

Mary Magdalene: Twin Flame and Divine Partner of Jesus. Ancient Egyptian Priestess. High initiate from the Pleiades, Venus, and other high consciousness realms. Arrived at Earth with Yeshua in the Star of Bethlehem Lightship. Gave birth to the offspring of Jesus. This lineage is spread throughout the world.

maya: Illusion. Projecting and veiling power of Source. All that has form and name which tests our ability to see the all-pervasive divine consciousness that supports all manifestations.

meditation: Conscious focusing of the mind on a single object.

merkaba: Divine light vehicle in the auric field that gives one the ability to travel to the higher light realms. Introduced back to humanity through Elijah.

Michael: Archangel who protects and defends all levels of Creation and biological life.

mindfulness: The practice of bringing our life's gross and subtle manifestations into the light of our awareness to observe life in nonduality. Nondual awareness is the ability to see beyond the illusion of duality and see with the eyes of loving awareness.

Mother Mary: Cosmic divine being, a Master soul, who incarnated to give birth to Jesus. High priestess of Ancient Egypt and master teacher of the cosmic priestess arts.

multidimensional: Existing in multiple planes of consciousness, i.e., physical, etheric, mental, and various spiritual dimensions.

Multiverse/multiverse: Universes within universes creating the totality of Creation. What Jesus spoke of when he referred to his "Father's house with many mansions."

-N-

nadis: Pathways of subtle energy in the body. There are said to be 72,0000 that weave in and around the physical body.

New Earth: 1. Higher density light spectrum reality of the ascended Earth. 2. Kingdom of Heaven on Earth.

nirvanic consciousness: liberated consciousness which has transcended suffering, limited egoic identity, and karmic cycles.

-O-

Orion: Constellation with ancient intelligent races with varying levels of consciousness and ranges of polarity. Factions of Reptilian and humanoid beings from Orion fought against Lyrans in the long galactic war.

oversoul: Higher consciousness identity of a soul. Where your individual soul comes from. Collective consciousness of myriad life streams and incarnations. 4th Density/5D Self.

-P-

past life regression: Form of hypnosis or shamanic journeying that evokes information from a client's subconscious mind from previous lifetimes.

Pleiadians: Star beings from the constellation of Pleiades, a highly advanced light consciousness school in our great universe. Cousins of humanity. They implanted upgraded DNA in humanity to open our spiritual connection.

prayer: Approach to the Divine through thought or word which opens the pathways for the living Light to infuse the one who is praying with love and divine insight.

priest: Male devotee of the Divine in service to the illumination of collective consciousness and the ascension of humanity. Administers the will and knowledge of the divine upon the Earth as well as the regenerative, healing presence of the divine feminine.

priestess: Female devotee of the Divine. Often connected to the Goddess. Embodies the wisdom of the divine feminine mothering principle of the Godhead. Matures consciousness in the community into higher states of creativity, sensuality, and grace.

psychic: One who has extrasensory perception. See *intuition*.

pyramids: Sacred architectural sites around the Earth built by various extraterrestrial and ultraterrestrial beings connecting the pathways of vital energy of the Earth with the universal energy grid for the reprogramming of life upon planet Earth. Act as broadcast and receiving systems for information used for planetary evolution.

Prakriti: Manifested reality, transactional reality as opposed to Absolute Reality, maya.

Purusha: Indwelling witness of Creation, Absolute Reality, Brahman, Pure Consciousness. Source Consciousness.

-Q-

quantum: Dealing with the holographic reality and fabric of Consciousness and creation.

quantum consciousness: Holographic consciousness connecting to the matrix of Creation with the ability to focus across time and space through nonlocality and consciousness projection.

quantum healing: Rapid, multidimensional healing that works at the cellular and subtle levels to bring the body's systems into homeostasis. Can be done through psychic processes, shamanic and energy medicine practices, hypnosis, quantum healing technology, star technology, and divine emanations. This is the medicine of New Earth.

quantum mysticism: Emerging evolutionary synthesis between science, metaphysics, and spirituality used to understand Consciousness and the laws that govern Creation.

Qumran: Ancient, multigenerational esoteric Essene community by the Dead Sea in present-day Israel that lived in complete recognition of the Divine through the study and embodiment of divine mystery teachings. Secretive community with advanced star knowledge and superhuman spiritual abilities. Traded knowledge with other global mystery schools and was home and school to Yeshua, Jesus of Nazareth. Yeshua's children studied here as well.

-R-

Reiki: 1. Japanese word meaning spiritual intelligence life force. 2. Intelligently-encoded, divine, redemptive, and regenerative energy from Source. 3. A gift of the Holy Spirit.

Redemption Plan: Cosmic and galactic initiative to restore humanity and Earth back to 4th Density as in the times of Lemuria. Includes genetic implantation, restoration of planetary grid, and operatives incarnating as human to bring new ideas and technologies, broadcasting intelligent and spiritual coding into the biofield of Earth and humanity, and more.

Reptilians: Reptilian humanoid star beings who have had a "negative" influence on Earth who have mostly evolved to positive polarity. Humans have reptilian DNA that gives us our ego mind to assist our perseverance in evolving.

reincarnation: The act of being born again into a new lifestream for the purpose of spiritual growth.

resonance: In spiritual terms, harmonic, synchronous vibrations between two or more objects.

Raphael: Archangel who administers to healing.

-S-

sacred sexuality: Alchemical sexual expression with the intention of uniting with the divine through one's own erotic spiritual nature. Can be practiced alone or with a partner(s).

sacred sites: Holy power spots spread across the planet that form a web of vortex points for subtle energy pathways of the Earth.

samsara: 1. Wheel of Karma 2. rounds and rounds of incarnations on the path of Ascension 3. Suffering mind. 4. Cycles of suffering.

samskaras: Grooves in the mind that create reactive emotions forming our biases, habits, and tendencies. Can be seen as negative or positive.

Self: Divine Self as opposed to the egoic self which is trapped in worldly conditioning.

sentience: The ability to feel, be conscious, or have one's own subjective experience.

service-to-all: Positively polarized, dedicated intention, thought, and action towards the Greater Good and Higher Love as an extension of one's True Self.

service-to-self: Negatively polarized, gives power to false self, ego. Can seem "positive" as intentions can be different than presentation.

sin: Intention, thought, and action that goes against one's inner light that causes an immediate depletion of life force and positive vibration. Serves the egoic self. There is no judgment for this from higher realms. All is for learning and growth. 2. Fear-based judgment system created by religion which connects to belief systems that limit the indwelling of spiritual light by creating perpetual states of fear, shame, and guilt. 3. The fundamental illusion of separation from Source.

Sirians: Star beings from the region of the Sirius A and Sirius B binary star system who have a long, positive history with humanity and are assisting Earth now.

Solaris: Central sun and stargate of our solar system which emanates supraliminal coding for the evolution of the myriad lifeforms in our solar system.

soul: 1. Subtle bodies which transmigrate from one life to the next. See *lightbody.*

spiritual partnership: A relationship that is supported by the desire to assist one another in awakening and healing.

soul contracts: Pre-designed plan and agreements before incarnating for the balancing of karma to propel the path of liberation and ascension. Includes soul agreements between individual souls to play out certain catalyst roles.

soul purpose: Divine intention for a soul for its incarnation encompassing the themes to be explored and lessons to be learned throughout a lifestream. Generally, a soul's purpose is to awaken to Higher Love and Divine Truth.

sovereign: natural consciousness state of the Atman/Self/Inner Source. Human beings embody and reclaim sovereignty through involution and higher consciousness evolution. Able to have agency in all areas of life. Self-regulated. Self-governed.

stargate: Portal used for transportation between long distances and different dimensions.

Star Nations: Space-traveling intelligent species, some positive, some negative, some neutral in relation to humanity and the Earth.

starseeds: Visitors from other schools in the multiverse who have volunteered to live a human life to assist the Ascension of Gaia and humanity. Many of which have experienced ascension mastery in other lifetimes. The best ascension masters from the universe are here on the planet or around the planet in crafts at this time.

substratum: 1. Foundational, base material 2. Source/Brahman/Atman/Pure Consciousness.

superluminal: 1. faster than light

synchronicity: The meeting of two or more seemingly unrelated events or objects that come together in a meaningful way that could even be perceived as divinely coordinated.

-T-

timelines: Pathways of probable events. Infinite potentials and realities fractal out and converge at particular junction points in "time" where choice points exist for the next fractal offshoots of timeline potentials. We are currently moving with multiple timeline potentials for Ascension events that lead to one inevitable event, 4th/5th Density New Earth. Timelines are constantly in flux depending on personal moment-to-moment choices from individuals or the collective meaning the future is never "fixed" but is always in flux. This is the reason why some psychics see different potential probabilities playing out in the future.

3D: Standard human consciousness in its unawakened state, fear/duality-based consciousness which is heavily programmed and hypnotized by the false matrix, the conditioning of the world, and the mind control techniques from the Archons.

Elders: Highest divine council. Progenitors of all cultures in the multiverse.

Twin Flames: Emanations of the same oversoul who assist one another in Ascension. Often uniting at the end of karmic cycles to serve Consciousness. Most commonly thought of as two people in Divine Partnership, but there can be more.

-U-V-W-Y-

Unified Field: The hologram of Creation, the Quantum Field, where all energies and manifestations arise from connecting all through Source Consciousness.

ultraterrestrial: Beings from beyond the physical plane, higher density beings in higher density forms.

vibration: The invisible, subtle layers of matter that form the basic templates for physical reality through repetitive oscillation.

Wisdom: Insight into the Divine Mysteries of Creation and the Godhead that connects us with higher states of divine love and divine grace. See *Knowledge, gnosis.*

walk-in: Exchange of souls during an incarnation. Typically occurs when the original soul consciousness assigned to the body can no longer continue an incarnation from trauma or some other way of vital depletion. A fresh soul consciousness is brought in to accomplish a certain task. Frequently used to bring highly developed galactic beings into the Earth for mission-oriented tasks.

Yeshua ben Joseph: See *Jesus* and *Christ*.

Recommended Reading

The Three Waves of Volunteers and The New Earth by Dolores Cannon
They Walked with Jesus by Dolores Cannon
Jesus and the Essenes by Dolores Cannon
Between Death and Life by Dolores Cannon
Keepers of The Garden by Dolores Cannon
Five Lives Remembered by Dolores Cannon
Return of the Bird Tribes by Ken Carey
Anna: Grandmother of Jesus by Claire Heartsong
Light on Life by B.K.S. Iyengar
The Yoga Sutras of Patanjali (many translations available)
Living Buddha, Living Christ by Thich Nhat Hahn
Reconciliation: Healing the Inner Child by Thich Nhat Hahn
Peace is Every Step by Thich Nhat Hahn
The Path of Energy by Dr. Synthia Andrews
The Seat of the Soul by Gary Zukav
The Book of Knowing and Worth by Paul Selig
The Diamond in Your Pocket by Gangaji
The Magdalen Manuscript: The Alchemies of Horus & the Sex Magic of Isis by Tom Kenyon and Judi Sion
The Kybalion by Three Initiates
Aparokshanubhuti by Adi Shankara
The Upanishads
The Bhagavad Gita
Drig Drishya Viveka
The Keys of Enoch by J.J. Hurtak
Pistis Sophia translated by J.J. Hurtak
The Secret Doctrine by H.P. Blavatsky
Etheric Double by A.E. Powell
The Causal Body and the Ego by A.E. Powell
Regression: Past-life Therapy for Here and Now by Samuel Sagan
Entity Possession: Freeing the Energy Body of Negative Influences by Samuel Sagan

THE ILLUMINATION CODEX

THE ILLUMINATION CODEX
GATEWAY ONE

Ascension Initiation

Keys for Higher Evolution

MICHAEL GARBER

THE ILLUMINATION CODEX
GATEWAY TWO PART ONE

Quantum Origins

Keys for Ancient Cosmology

MICHAEL GARBER

THE ILLUMINATION CODEX
GATEWAY TWO PART TWO

Cosmic Christ Transmissions

The Ministry of Light

MICHAEL GARBER

THE ILLUMINATION CODEX
GATEWAY FOUR

Chakra Yoga Discourse

Keys for Higher Consciousness

MICHAEL GARBER

THE ILLUMINATION CODEX
GATEWAY TWO PART THREE

New Earth Transmissions

Future Timelines of Gaia

MICHAEL GARBER

THE ILLUMINATION CODEX
GATEWAY THREE

Path of Awakening

Keys for Transfiguration

MICHAEL GARBER

THE ILLUMINATION CODEX
GATEWAY FIVE

Laying of Hands
Reiki & Beyond

MICHAEL GARBER

WWW.NEWEARTHASCENDING.ORG

Support Our Initiatives

Ron and I have dedicated our lives to supporting this Grand Transition. We stand alongside all of you as humanity awakens to its True Nature and becomes a People of Light in the heavenly reality of New Earth.

New Earth Ascending is dedicated to assisting people to realize their divinity and manifest that truth in every aspect of their life. For more information about New Earth Ascending or to contact Michael, please scan the QR code below for a list of resources and links, or visit *www.newearthascending.org*. Be sure to check out our courses including the Illuminated Quantum Healing practitioner course.

New Earth Ascending is a registered 508 (c)(1)(a) Self-Supported Non-profit Church Ministry with a global outreach. We greatly appreciate your support as we create new systems, communities, and schools for the development of the New Earth civilization. If you would like to make a tax-deductible donation to support our mission, please go to:

https://donorbox.org/donationtonewearthascending

Scan with a smart device camera for more information including websites, social media, and more! Bless us all!

www.ingramcontent.com/pod-product-compliance
Lightning Source LLC
Chambersburg PA
CBHW071357120626
46546CB00002B/731